PASTORAL COUNSELING IN SOCIAL PROBLEMS:
extremism, race, sex, divorce

1368

BY
WAYNE E. OATES

The Westminster Press
Philadelphia

Published by The Westminster Press ®
Philadelphia, Pennsylvania

PRINTED IN THE UNITED STATES OF AMERICA

To PAULINE

My Joint Heir of the Grace of Life
and the Guardian of My Solitude

CONTENTS

PREFACE

Pastoral care risks the hyperindividualism of some forms of evangelism that ignore the great social dilemmas out of which individual problems of persons emerge. This book is written to offset this danger in the mind and practice of the pastor.

I am indebted to President J. McDowell Richards and the Faculty of the Columbia Theological Seminary at Decatur, Georgia, for their invitation to deliver these chapters as the 1965 Smyth Lectures. Their kindness and the receptiveness of the entire seminary community has been a powerful source of encouragement in the effort to perfect these lectures.

These lectures have been written during a time of enforced confinement because of major spinal surgery. I am indebted to Walter Coe, M.D., my personal physician, John Ivins, M.D., and Alfred Uihlein, M.D., of Mayo Clinic, for their expert treatment and convalescent care of me, which freed me of pain that without their wisdom and care would have prevented this book from being written. I am debtor also to my wife who has been the instrument of God's grace in the long days and nights when apart from her presence I would have been unable to face life, much less to function creatively as a writer. She has taught me what the vow to care for me in sickness and health really means.

Mrs. Richard Landon, my secretary, has demonstrated highly efficient research assistance and secretarial ability in the production of this manuscript. Her competence and commitment have both perfected and hastened the completion of the task.

I owe a special debt of gratitude also to President Duke McCall and to Dean Penrose St. Amant of the Southern Baptist Theological Seminary for providing both the kind of teaching situation and the advantage of full-time secretarial assistance that enabled me to reflect upon and set down these thoughts.

W. E. O.

Louisville, Kentucky

CHAPTER 1

PASTORAL COUNSELING AND THE PROPHETIC
TASK

IN 1950 I asked a young German theological student in
New York why it was that pastors on the European Con-
tinent and in Great Britain had not at that time taken pastoral care and counseling as seriously as had American pastors. He replied that the troubles of Germans and Britons in
postwar years were massive. The things that had happened
to them as nations were catastrophic. The Germans tended
to think of individual troubles as trivial. Alan Paton, in his
Cry, the Beloved Country, said that the chieftains of South
Africa were counselors in many things, but that they had
no counsel for the brokenness of their people.

In the mid-sixties, pastoral care and counseling has become a more regularized part of the theological curriculum
in many schools. Several student generations have been
graduated into active pastoral roles. Yet, intentionally or
not, the work of the pastor as a counselor and as a caring
person has been taught and learned as a highly individual
work of pastors in purely one-to-one relationships with people. Occasionally some objecting voice puts in a plea for the
pulpit work of the pastor, superficially equating this with
the prophetic task of the pastor. Pastoral care cannot so
easily be separated from the social context in which the
counseling takes place. Nor can the quiet encounter of a
private conference with an individual or a small group be

so easily excluded from the work of the prophet. The private ministry of the pastor cannot be nonchalantly cut loose from his public ministry. Pastoral care itself involves the pastor in the social dilemmas of the neighborhood, community, city, county, state, nation. International situations and events that surround the pastor and his people affect the work of caring. Willingly or unwillingly, the pastor is caught in the maelstrom of human suffering that defies analysis, repudiates reason, and demands decisions.

The purpose, therefore, of this book is to discuss the role and function of the pastor in the context of several contemporary social dilemmas. The present crisis of extremism, the continuing dilemma of ministering to divorced persons, the social dilemmas of the race issue, the recurrent demands for pastoral care in institutional conflict, and the major challenges to a Christian sexual ethic today are massive social dilemmas that consume much of the working day of the caring pastor. Specific focus upon them does not appear to any great extent in the literature of pastoral care. Responses to papers delivered on these subjects convince me that a book devoted to such concerns not only is needed but is badly needed at this time. It probably will be needed for some time to come. The reciprocity between the pastoral caring and the prophetic confronting of responsibilities of the contemporary minister is the core concern of this book.

The Pastor as Prophet

The patient application of the clinical method in pastoral care has taught us many things that illuminate the minister's responsibility to be a prophet of the living God. Clinical pastoral work recaptures neglected and omitted aspects of the Biblical portraits of the prophets. It challenges easy clichés today as to what it means to be prophetic. Clinical pastoral care omits neither the responsibility of the pastor as a prophet nor leaves the stereotypes of the prophetic role unchallenged. Both the omissions and the stereotypes have to go when the pastor takes his responsibilities in pastoral care seriously and attends to their social expression in the life of the church and community.

Stereotypes of the Pastor as Prophet

Stereotype images of the pastor as a prophet must be identified. The first stereotype is that of the prophet as a tactless, loud-spoken, fist-waving, authoritarian bully who browbeats people into submission to his point of view. This is often considered as "being directive." Persons who are "nondirective" and "client-centered" in their approach to pastoral care, therefore, shrink from such "prophecy." A second stereotype is that of the preacher who makes the pulpit his opportunity to "take a stand," to state his position heedless of the opinions and "stands" of other people. He makes these "stands" on a take-it-or-leave-it basis. Pastors who do this are identified by many people as "prophets." However, this removes responsibility from the pastor for two-way communication between the prophet and his audience. A third stereotype is that of the prophet as the "cleanser of the temple." With the knotted cords he lashes people for their wrongheadedness. The incident recorded in the Scripture of the Lord Jesus Christ is used as proof text for this stereotype. It is taken out of the context of the rest of the ministry of Jesus. A fourth stereotype of the prophet is that of the modern "angry young man" who loses his job because of his convictions. He is eager to be fired. Exact parallels are drawn between this person and the prophets of the Old Testament and the "crucifixion" of Jesus. The fact that the prophets of the Old Testament were not paid employees and that the crucifixion of Jesus had nothing to do with the loss of a job in a power struggle is not made a part of the picture of the prophet. A fifth stereotype of the prophet over-simplifies issues by sharp black and white antitheses that leave out the ambiguities of the intermediate gray issues. This removes the element of tragedy from the genuine pro-phetic situation. The humanity of the prophet is omitted. That he prophesies in part is not recognized in the proph-ecy. A sixth stereotype of the prophet is the "face value" that is put upon his word. It is to be taken without being tested, authenticated, and tried. Yet the Biblical witness never extols prophecy for prophecy's sake. True and false prophets are to be distinguished from each other. Prophecy fails. We prophesy in part. Prophecy is transcended in faith, hope, and love. Our finiteness, limitation, ambiguity, and weakness are the ground of real humility in the prophet. Confidence in God who is love puts the minister as a prophet in perspective.

Clinical pastoral approaches to the ministry challenge these stereotypes. The tactless, loud-spoken, fist-waving au-thoritarian bully portrays his own insecurity more than the prophetic wisdom of God. The confident and secure pastor deals with controversial situations in policy-setting sessions with his lay leadership when both he and they can set forth their points of view in dialogue. When he preaches, he ex-tends the invitation of Isaiah to come and reason together concerning the great social dilemmas and the intentions of God in them. The pastor who understands himself refrains from equating his own methods of confrontation with Jesus' cleansing of the Temple. He does not make a test case of his own job. He bears the hurt of his people with them in talking with them individually as well as collectively. He knows that a social issue is a *dilemma,* filled with ambiguity, self-deception, confusion, and contradiction. He sees himself as a minister of reconciliation. He maintains enough objectivity to see the dilemmas of his people steadily and to see them whole. He strives for enough independence of judgment to minister to people of widely varying points of view. He is not afraid of the loneliness that this ministry of reconciliation inevitably entails.

The stereotypes of prophecy are also countermanded in Biblical perspectives of the prophet. Nathan did not scream to a great crowd in his prophetic confrontation of David. He spoke to him privately in a parable and applied it in a quiet voice. Jeremiah was asked for guidance by Zedekiah and apparently saw him in privacy and without authoritarian fanfare. Unlike the second stereotype, the apostle Paul rarely had a pulpit from which to preach, contending instead with people in the marketplace in vigorous two-way question-and-answer sessions. Or when he was not doing this, he was teaching consecutively and deliberately to groups of inquirers, as at Ephesus. The prophets and the apostles were sometimes lashed, but they themselves seldom resorted to dramatic shows of force as the " temple cleansers " do. Unlike the angry young man of today, they could not lose their jobs, for they had not been employed in the first place! These Biblical prophets wrestled and contended with themselves and with God, searching for the truth of their own message and seeking to be directed and led by God. They identified themselves with their people in bondage, and when their people were hurt, they were hurt. They were capable of empathy as well as courage, tender concern as well as stern rebuke.

Temptations of the Contemporary Pastor as a Prophet

In the presence of the confusion of stereotyped community expectations and the self-expectations of pastors as prophets, temptations abound for the pastor himself. These stereotypes "set him up" like a bowling pin for several major temptations that lurk in the glare of these stereotyped pictures of the pastor as prophet.

The temptation to exhibitionism. Every pastor has a streak of the ham actor in him. He tucks it away smugly enough, but it emerges when an opportunity for showmanship presents itself. The great social dilemmas of which we shall speak in the following chapters tempt him to be "the hero," to show off, and to satisfy his own exhibitionistic needs. Crisis situations call the "knight on the white charger" impulse out of a pastor. He jumps on his horse and rides off madly in six directions! The need for a person to prove that he is not "chicken," that he is "brave," and to make "prophetic faces" before a crowd is not the private impulse of teen-agers daring each other to steal a car in which some adult has left the keys. Social dilemmas present the same temptation to exhibitionism to the pastor and the teacher in a time of acute social crisis.

The temptation to publicity. Allied with the temptation to exhibitionism is the need for publicity. Mass media of communication both facilitate and impede social change in their reporting of such social dilemmas as the race conflicts of our day, the major calamities that befall masses of people, and the personal tragedies connected with such events as divorce and other socially conflictual situations. When the story "gets in the papers" or "on the radio" or "on television," the problems which were simply added to each other up to that point become multiplied by each other from this time forward. The lunge for publicity does not leave the pastor untouched. The recent news accounts of a Catholic priest ministering to the dying in a hospital fire graphically express the correct stance of the Christian pastor of every persuasion in the face of the temptation to publicity. A picture showed the priest with his back to the camera as he held a burned victim in his arms. The caption beneath said simply: " My God, no! I am busy! " This was his answer to a newsman who had asked him if he had any comment to make and what his name was. One of the contributions of the medical profession to the modern practice of pastoral care has been the studious avoidance of publicity in behalf of the healing ministry. The minister of reconciliation seeks a way of transcendence of social conflict. He resists the temptation of publicity.

The temptation to one-way thinking. The minister of reconciliation bases his work on both the reversal of the processes of conflict and the development of two-way communication. In order to do this, he must seek consultation, encourage negotiation between conflicting interests and intentions, and nurture the willingness to be reconciled. In his own way of life, therefore, he does not mistake deadlines, ultimatums, and ex-cathedra pronouncements for the essence of prophecy. On the contrary, he *contends* with people, leaving the whole burden of breaking communication upon them. If the efforts at understanding, reason, commitment, and resolution of difficulty are to stop, the other persons will have to do the stopping. President O. T. Binkley, of Southeastern Baptist Theological Seminary, together with a prominent psychoanalyst, was on a panel discussing religion and psychoanalysis. The analyst had said that the more completely a patient recovered from his illness, the more the analyst tended to part company with religion. President Binkley said: " If there is to be a parting of the way between an effective Christian pastor and an effective psychoanalyst in the treatment of the patient, the Christian pastor will depend upon the analyst to do the parting. It is the role of the Christian pastor to stay with the analyst until *he* leaves *him!*" When psychotherapists juxtapose themselves over against the Christian faith or any other form of religion, the clergyman is faced with a dilemma, namely, that of rejecting the philosophical presuppositions of his opponent and at the same time affirming the verifiable clinical data of the psychotherapists.

The temptation to play God. The ultimate temptation of the pastor as a prophet is no different from any other temptation to sin. This is the temptation to take God's place. The question that Joseph asked himself and his brothers in the face of their injustices to him was: " Am I in God's place? " The social prophet, the pastor who crusades for a cause, or the pastor who works quietly out of sight behind the scenes as a minister of reconciliation should ask himself this same question every morning so that he may walk humbly and every night so that he may sleep calmly: " Am I in God's place? " Then he will resist the temptation to mistake his ability to prophesy, to crusade, to work behind the scenes for the absolute power of work, acting to settle the destinies of all men. Then he will know in part and prophesy in part. He takes the ambiguity of his cause upon himself and moves with a measure of compassion even toward his worst opponent. He remains open to negotiation, to reconciliation, to peace.

Principles of Prophetic Pastoral Care

These stereotypes and temptations of the prophetic pastor are like a negative film. We are now in a position to use this negative to develop a positive print of the basic principles that should guide the pastor in exercising the prophetic ministry.

Balance Between Visibility and Invisibility
in Pastoral Practice

A careful study of parishioner expectations of pastors made by Glock and Roos revealed that parishioners tend to form their expectations of pastors on the basis of what they *see* the pastors do. The pastor as a counselor is not seen. He jeopardizes his work as a counselor unless he provides an atmosphere of privacy and trusted communication for those who seek his help. His private negotiations with leaders in a community controversy — such as a church controversy, a race conflict, a contention for the mind of a parishioner being pulled by two sets of extremists — go unseen and unpublicized by his parishioners and outsiders as well. He has, therefore, two temptations: He can play dead and do nothing in the social dilemmas of his community or he can protest that he is misunderstood and begin to advertise his " good works " as a private counselor and negotiator between controversial people. Public opinion tends to damn him in either instance.

The success of a pastor in resolving social conflicts is greatest, however, when a productive solution of the conflict is reached with little or no connection with his name or with no " credit " being given him.

The New Testament injunction about almsgiving can be transferred to the pastoral attitude toward social justice and social action: " Beware of practicing your piety before men in order to be seen by them; for then you will have no reward from your Father who is in heaven. Thus, when you give alms, sound no trumpet before you, as the hypocrites do in the synagogues and in the streets, that they may be praised by men. Truly, I say to you, they have their reward. But when you give alms, do not let your left hand know what your right hand is doing, so that your alms may be in secret; and your Father who sees in secret will reward you " (Matt. 6:1-4). Keeping one's own left hand uninformed as to the activity of the right hand in social action calls for discipline on the part of the prophet himself as well as his discipline of his followers' demand that he be seen by them.

This is no new principle of the Christian life. When great social dilemmas become the domain of imperialistic extremists, Christian witnesses have been forced into anonymity. In many parts of the world today, the Christian pastor is only a stone's throw from the condition of early Christians who wrote their sign *ichthys* in the sand and utilized the elaborate symbolism of the book of Revelation as a means of subverbal communication with each other. They put more " between " the lines than " in " the lines. The Christian pastor can neither use his unseenness as a cloak for compromise nor feel too sorry for himself when other ministers who are more removed from the scene of battle complain because he does not hold daily news conferences, issue great statements, and circulate petitions. He must see himself as waging guerrilla warfare for the Kingdom of God, known neither by uniform nor headline and rewarded only in secret.

The contemporary pastor's earned identity as a trained counselor, both with individuals and with small groups, particularly equips him to implement the " invisible " ministry of the Christian pastor. The effective pastor facing social dilemmas can use his role as a personal counselor, spiritual director, and small-group leader to leaven the whole social process of his community. He no longer has to depend entirely upon mass structures and public utterances to implement his prophetic vision of the City of God among men. He no longer needs whole divisions of the structures of the church to effect major social changes. The dialogue of the personal interview and the give-and-take of small-group discussion can bring more than pronouncements from the minister. It can bring insight and commitment to both the minister and parishioner. Both develop a "tailored" understanding that deals with each other's biases and clarifies each other's purposes and positions. Neither is closed to the depersonalization and collectivization of "crowd" minds.

The personal interview and the small-group conference are certainly not the only means of effecting social change in the face of cultural dilemmas. They are the central means of pastoral care and yet the ones most likely to be neglected when any social issue — alcoholism, divorce, race, extremism, and war — becomes a celebrated "single issue" definition of human life and the mind of God. If the pastor neglects his ministry to individuals and to small groups, he may be sure that extremists will take over this function for their own purposes when a social conflict reaches fever stage. Then he will defensively bemoan the development of a "Protestant underground" that perverts personal interviews and small-group conferences into the use of anonymous phone calls, threatening by unsigned letters, etc., and brainwashing all group techniques that delete the sovereignty of God and the ministry of the Holy Spirit.

Prophetic Acts and Pastoral Care

Superficial marketplace understandings of prophetic pastoral work are restricted to things the pastor *says,* pronouncements he makes, "stands" he takes, "white papers" he issues, and petitions he signs. The reverse side of this coin is the tendency of those both within and without the church to depreciate the worth of the spoken sermon. Biblical perspectives of the prophet and the apostle, however,

focus not upon formal sermons, written documents, and
"problem-centered" pronouncements but upon their acts
and relationships. It is not by chance that Luke's account of
the early church and the work of the apostles is not entitled "Sermons by Peter and Paul" but "The Acts of the
Apostles."

In the Old Testament the symbolic acts of the prophets
and the intense relationships they had to the power structures of their day were the conduit for the transmission of
their identity as prophets. One among many examples may
be cited. Jeremiah, in his early prophetic experience (Jer.
8:4-7), conducted a "listening-in campaign" in order to get
at the root of the troubles of his people. He wanted to know
why it was that when men fell, they did not get up, why
when they missed the way, they did not turn around. He
was concerned about their persistent desertion. Consequently, he developed the prophetic act of "listening in." He
says in Jer. 8:6: "I have given heed and listened." He was
able to listen as well as to speak and he formulated his prophetic message on the basis of hearing as well as of saying.

Another incident in Jeremiah's prophetic work illustrates
the art of portraying a prophetic message in an act rather
than in a speech. In Jer. 13:1-11 he says that he went and
bought himself a girdle and put it on his loins, taking care
not to let it go into the water. He then took the girdle and
hid it in the cleft of the rock in the Euphrates River. Thus
he acted out a parable. The girdle was the kind that the
priests wore ceremonially. It represented Judah, the people
of God. The girdle is the principal ornament of the Orien-
tal man, worn close to his body. It represents the closeness
and intimacy of the covenant of God with his people.
It represents something "prized and intimate, a thing of
dignity and beauty." When Jeremiah took this prized garment of high symbolic value and "buried it below the sur-

face in the rocky water-drenched river bank," he drama-
tized what was happening to the religious covenant between God and his people. That which was most prized
by them was saturated with a river of idolatrous influence
and gradually permeated them as well. At length they were
made "good for nothing" (Elmer A. Leslie, *Jeremiah*, pp.
85-87; Abingdon Press, 1954).

Today pastors are called upon to do prophetic things. A
young Tennessee pastor, when his small city was in the
throes of a race conflict over the integration of the local
schools, made few if any speeches. Rather, on the morning
that the tension was at its highest pitch, he made a prophetic decision to act. He went to the "nigger town" where
the children who had been enrolled in school lived. He
asked them for the privilege of walking to school with them.
They permitted him to do so, and he walked the long fear-
ridden distance with the Negro children. He was mauled
and beaten by those who opposed the enrollment of Negroes in a previously all-white school. But he got his message through by a prophetic act.

Face-to-Faceness and Prophetic Behavior

A second principle of prophetic and apostolic behavior in
the presence of the great social dilemmas of today is the
principle of "face-to-faceness." Enemies cannot be reconciled *in absentia* without couriers. Couriers have needs of
their own. Couriers can confuse rather than clarify communication. The objective of prophetic pastoral care is to
produce a face-to-face, firsthand relationship and to reduce
indirect, secondhand attempts to manipulate and manage
people from afar. The psalmist says that the Lord prepares
a table for him in the presence of his enemies. The absence
of the enemy makes him more an enemy.

The estranged husband and wife come to a level of

" blackout " on communication. Then go-betweens begin to do their information-getting, opinion-conveying, and attitude-expressing for them. The pastor who falls into this work for them becomes a part of the problem rather than a part of the solution. The alienated races in a community have few lines of face-to-face communication. Their attitudes are formed on the basis of hearsay and courier-gained information. Not the least of these is information gained through newspapers. Newspapers can be divided into two groups: those which attempt to improve communication within a communication and those which exploit failures of communication and thereby magnify conflict. Occasionally the newsman rises to the level of his moral responsibility by improving communications. Occasionally ministers also do the same thing. When they do, they become prophetic, regardless of their occupational " estate." The ministry of reconciliation *intends* to get people into face-to-face conversation with each other.

This does not always mean that " sweetness and light " will ensue. Even if we use the conjoint approach to treating, the situation will itself deteriorate. If, however, an intention of removing distortions of communication, misinformation, and inadequate information can be the purpose of such face-to-face confrontations, then the basis for later, more peaceful conversations can be laid. We need go no farther than the relationship of the apostle Paul and the apostle Peter to see the sharp contention that arose over eating with Gentiles. This is recorded in Gal. 2:11-12. Paul says: " When Cephas came to Antioch I opposed him to his face, because he stood condemned." This face-to-faceness led to a higher resolution of the social conflict, a resolution that could not have taken place if Paul and Peter had relied upon what other people said to them about each other. The

Jerusalem conference on the same issue of the relationship between Jews and Gentiles may have preceded the confrontation between Paul and Peter. The problem upon which they disagreed, and in which Barnabas was also implicated, had been dealt with in the conference; a " position " letter had been written by the combined group and was publicized throughout the churches (see Acts 15:22-29). I am indebted to my colleague, Dr. Harold Songer, professor of New Testament, for the following commentary on the Gal. 2:1-10 passage and other related passages:

> The theory that the letter to the Galatians was sent to the churches in South Galatia opens the possibility that the dispute described in Gal. 2:11-14 preceded the Apostolic Conference in Acts, ch. 15. On this theory, Gal. 2:1-10 may be correlated with Acts 11:27-30 rather than Acts, ch. 15. Some modern scholars hold this view. Cf. Archibald M. Hunter, *Interpreting the New Testament, 1900-1950* (The Westminster Press, 1952), pp. 65-66.
>
> Most scholars, however, hold that Gal. 2:1-10 should be correlated with Acts, ch. 15. This reconstruction of the sequence of events would make Peter's visit to Antioch subsequent to the Jerusalem Conference. Cf. Floyd V. Filson, *A New Testament History: The Story of the Emerging Church* (The Westminster Press, 1964), pp. 224-225.
>
> But even before the conference in Acts, ch. 15, the basic issue emerges in a semiofficial conference in Acts 11:1-18. In Acts, ch. 10, Peter ate with Gentiles as he did later in Antioch. The Jerusalem Church was disturbed by Peter's conduct, but approved it. (Acts 11:1-18.) Apparently it takes more than one confrontation for some people to see the issues! Peter seems to have had two positions after Acts, ch. 15. When his status was threatened by representatives of the Jerusalem Church (Gal. 2:12), he segregated himself from Gentiles; but when he was in a context that did not challenge his loyalty to James, he could integrate comfortably.
>
> It is hard to determine where Peter really stood. In

Acts, ch. 10, he initiates contact with a Gentile; in Acts, ch. 15, he reminds the Jerusalem Christians of this and speaks for integration; but in Antioch a short while after this, he at first stands on one side, then on the other (Gal. 2:12).

This was not enough, though. That which had been set forth in the encyclical still had to be dealt with on the personal and pastoral level, *even among those who had been in the meeting and helped write the letter*. There was no substitute then nor is there now for personal and small-group working through of social dilemmas.

The early church's experience along this line was summed up in the report in Matt., ch. 18, of the *modus operandi* of face-to-face handling of ethical issues that involve social conflict and call for confrontation. The three-step levels of pastoral and personal action are staged as follows:

If your brother sins against you, go and tell him his fault, between you and him alone. If he listens to you, you have gained your brother. But if he does not listen, take one or two others along with you, that every word may be confirmed by the evidence of two or three witnesses. If he refuses to listen to them, tell it to the church; and if he refuses to listen even to the church, let him be to you as a Gentile and a tax collector. Truly, I say to you, whatever you bind on earth shall be bound in heaven, and whatever you loose on earth shall be loosed in heaven. (Matt. 18:15-18.)

Yet this cannot be done on a simple horizontal man-to-man basis without the whole process becoming a test of courage, a test of strength, and an attempt to " prove one's manhood and prowess." This must be done with the awareness of the presence of God, in the quest for the instruction of the Holy Spirit, and with a full intention to see what it is that is in need of forgiveness. It is in the same context that the promise of Jesus is recorded:

> Again I say to you, if two of you agree on earth about everything they ask, it will be done for them by my Father in heaven. For where two or three are gathered in my name, there am I in the midst of them. (Matt. 18:19-20.)

The presence of the living Christ does not exclude the possibility of real social conflict. As in personal life, social conflict may be evidence of the radical work of the Holy Spirit bringing underlying infection to a head and healing the organism of the body of Christ. Social conflict may be the Holy Spirit's challenging a community to new growth. To hold on to old ways in the presence of new demands would destroy the community itself. As such, the Holy Spirit cannot be really known in the " sweetness and light " sentimentality of pietism. Social pain, like bodily pain, may be concomitant with healing and growth. Both are destructive when allowed to become a way of life rather than a means of grace under the sovereignty of God, in the fellowship of Christ, and under the tutelage of the Holy Spirit.

In contemporary social conflicts in which a pastor is called to function prophetically, however, the *modus operandi* of the New Testament just cited is rather consistently reversed. In the first place, we have come to depend too heavily on mimeographed letters and memoranda, public addresses, mass media of communication, and pronouncements of official bodies of both church and state to solve great social dilemmas. These can precede, follow, and implement personal and small group discussion on a face-to-face basis. They cannot replace it; they can only *seem* to replace it. In the second place, instead of reconciliation beginning with two offended parties on a face-to-face basis, it quite often begins by one or the other or both bringing the matter before a large group and publicly calling the other a heathen of some kind. Then it moves to two or three negotiators trying to " get them together and talk things out and help them to talk themselves together." These efforts are often doomed from the outset because of the hurt occasioned by the public " proclamations " and demonstrations of pseudoprophetic position-taking. If the matter ever gets to the one-to-one level of both personal candor and forgiveness, then the matter may have become so infected with social repercussions that a settled aversion and permanent hostility is the result.

Two-Way Communication and the Pastor as a Prophet

In popular thought within the ministry, pastoral care is overidentified with " listening," and prophetic utterance is overidentified with " speaking." A further principle of pastoral care and prophetic responsibility would reject both these popular assumptions. Both are one-way forms of communication. Neither is complete without the other. The pastor as a prophet who cares functions on the principle of two-way communication, dialogue and not monologue. The pastor should walk in Jeremiah's tradition of a listening-in campaign as a dialectical complement to his " utterance " ministry.

The best single treatment of this principle of pastoral care in the face of social dilemmas is Reuel Howe's book entitled *The Miracle of Dialogue*. Howe describes the purpose of dialogical communication as over against one-way communication. He does so both negatively as to what the purposes of communication are *not*, and he does so positively as to what the purposes of communication *are*. Communication is *not* giving *our* answers to people's questions. The pastor should use his knowledge, skill, and understanding in helping people to find answers of their own through the process of creative decision-making. Communication is *not* the process of getting total agreement among a group with the point of view of the communicator. Rather, the purpose of the communicator is to bring people with unique and profound differences into responsible " relation in which the uniqueness of each stands in a complementary relation to the other. And this is possible even when there is dis-agreement " (Reuel L. Howe, *The Miracle of Dialogue*, p. 56; The Seabury Press, Inc., 1963).

On the contrary, the positive objectives of communica-tion of a two-way dialogical are more that of the teacher than that of the exhorter and crusader. " Communication," says Howe, " is a means by which information and meaning is conveyed and received between individuals and groups." (*Ibid.*) The responsibility of the pastor as a prophet, there-fore, is to see to it that accurate information and a clear statement of issues are made abundantly available to those whom he leads. Facts and meanings fill the gap of ignorance and offset the growth of rumor and distortion. This calls for providential foresight on the part of the prophetic pas-tor in providing fact, experience, and meaning for those whom he leads long before opportunists, crusaders, extrem-ists, and other forms of demagogues. A demagogue is little concerned with real communication. By definition he is " one skilled in arousing the prejudices . . . of the popu-lace by rhetoric, sensational charges, specious arguments, catchwords, cajolery, etc.; especially a political speaker or leader who seeks thus to make capital of social discontent and incite the populace, usually in the name of some popu-lar cause, in order to gain political influence or office " (*Webster's New International Dictionary of the English*

Language, Second Edition, Unabridged, p. 694; G. & C. Merriam Company, Publishers, 1955).

A second positive purpose of communication is the encouragement of people in making responsible decisions "whether that decision be Yes or No in relation to the truth that is presented. . . . A decision to say No is as much a part of dialogue as a decision to say Yes" (Howe, *op. cit.,* p. 57). Two-way communication must of necessity be an open word. Rebellion against thoroughly true propositions or social stands often produces a vehement "No!" not because the rebel is opposed to the stand but because his own freedom of decision was removed from him in a one-way monologue. A characteristic of undisciplined and false prophecy is its removal of this freedom. The rebel on the other hand is likely to mistake his resentment against the removal of his freedom for a violent rejection of a genuinely good proposition. The most poignant example of this is the otherwise reasonable segregationist in the South today. Not all segregationists are "otherwise reasonable," but many of them are.

A final purpose of two-way communication is "to bring back the forms of life into relation to the vitality which produced them." In my estimate, the vitality that produces life is the unadulterated covenant with which a given relationship is formed. The marriage that is threatened by separation and divorce was earlier threatened by a withdrawal of the partners from open communication with each other. This was caused still earlier by the entrée of suspicion and distrust. Underneath this was a breach of the covenant that originally produced the marriage. A church conflict follows a similar loss of touch and relation to the covenant that brought it into being. This is the conscience struggle of the churches of the South, for example, on the race issue. Many such churches were formed on the basis of a covenant that assumed without discussion the principle of segregation. They were formed on a principle of localism and familism. Their leaders who attempt to be prophetic without going back with them to the basis of their covenant as a church, reexamining the forms of vitality that brought the church into being and doing so on the basis of two-way communication, will inevitably produce chaos. But the pastor who moves with his people on an open-ended reexamination of the nature of the church, the kind of covenant that binds it together, and the purpose of the church in the world will find a basis for the ministry of reconciliation on the social dilemma of race. However, he will be a pleasing sight neither to the irrational integrationist nor to the irrational segregationist. As one faithful pastor in the South put it, " The beatitude for the peacemaker should be revised to read: ' Blessed are the peacemakers, for they shall catch hell from both sides! ' "

The Principle of Clarification

The next principle of prophetic pastoral care is the principle of clarification. Personal counseling combines the act of listening and speaking on the part of the counselor. The counselor hears what the person is saying. He hears it together with him in such a way that what the counselee is saying and what the counselor is hearing are mutually agreed upon by both to be the same. The counselor clarifies *with* the counselee what is being said in terms of its meaning, not just its words. The same words can mean too many different things to leave at face value the meaning of the words being used.

The pastor has this same responsibility in his work with small groups and with the congregation as a whole. In this process the question becomes more effective than the answer. In small groups and in preaching opportunities, pastors have too often let the prophetic act of " the question for clarification " go undone in behalf of the less prophetic and easier task of " giving answers " with airtight logic. The pastor who does this is indebted more to Greek rhetoric than to the Hebrew prophets and apostles. Both the Old and the New Testaments give the lively interchange of vital questions between prophets and apostles on the one hand and those to whom they ministered on the other. The parable was told, the question asked, other questions asked, and the answer arrived at together. The incident — casual as could be, such as the questions of a lawyer, a rich young man, etc. — occurred. Questions were raised in the minds of the disciples. Only then were answers given. In other incidents already written answers in the Law were given, such as those about divorce. When the disciples then asked: " Would it not be better that people do not marry? " Jesus gave his answer.

The prophetic pastor today has the responsibility of clarifying the basic issues in social dilemmas such as extremism, divorce, race, sexual morality, etc. A certain open-endedness and invitation to discussion and dialogue must give atmosphere to such clarification, however; otherwise, the element of genuine two-way communication is destroyed. Even in situations where the pastor's authority is supinely relied upon " to do whatever he thinks best," as in the case of divorce, the pastor cannot let himself be charmed by power into doing as he pleases and speaking ex cathedra. He himself may learn something new if he takes time to talk personally and in small groups with persons vitally involved, and to involve people who should be more vitally related in the decision-making process. Nor can he wait until a test case appears before he clarifies the issues in social dilemmas.

However, the prophetic act of clarification and reconciliation can be interpreted by the pastor's hearers and followers as shilly-shallying between the two sides, as " not taking a stand," and as " straddling the fence " on important issues. If the pastor is a clever person and on other occasions has been guilty of manipulation, he is likely to be interpreted as being a " smooth operator " and as one who " plays both ends against the middle " to gain his own ends. In fact, these descriptions may be true, and the pastor must examine his own motives before God to assess the truth in such accusations. Without a clear covenant that defines the task of the pastor as that of a counselor amid conflict, the pastor easily becomes a Mr. Two-Positions who speaks smooth sayings to the particular persons he happens to be with at a given time. He becomes, in Bunyan's classical metaphor, " Mr. Facing-both-ways."

This can be avoided in social conflicts and dilemmas much as the marriage counselor avoids it with husbands and wives who are in open conflict with each other. He enters a covenant with them to be a pastor to both members of the partnership and not to " choose up sides " and " blame " one at the expense of the other. He commits himself to work at opening channels of communication between the contending sides with the objective of resolving the differences to the mutual advantage of both contenders. He refuses to be a courier or message bearer, but instead tries to encourage openness and trust between them. He himself moves on the assumption that the " truth " is not possessed solely by either contender but that it is " between " them. No one is to blame but everyone is responsible. Even with a covenant like this, forces of manipulation will seek to use and coerce the pastor. In massive social dilemmas, the pastor may himself be victimized and become expendable. His prophetic objective, however, is to put the whole community " on base," even if he himself is " thrown out " before he " gets to first base."

The Principle of Anticipation

The prophet in the Biblical account was often the seer, and the authenticity of his work as prophet rested at times on the extent to which his capacity to foresee situations proved to be good. Consequently, the prophets of the Old Testament, for example, were exceptionally keen observers of the course of personal and social history around them. Their grasp of the totality of these events was indeed both inspired by God and enriched by their own high intelligence, an intelligence committed to God. They could anticipate the shape of things to come and acted upon the ultimate possibilities of a given situation rather than the threats and opportunities of the situation itself. They rested their lives in God's hands to vindicate their interpretation of history.

The prophetic pastor today, in both personal and public ministry, must operate on a similar principle of farsighted appreciation of the shape of things to come. If he is to deal with social dilemmas effectively, he cannot wait until the issues at hand are confused by the opportunistic needs of the extremist, the baiters, and the demagogues. One way of anticipating social dilemmas in advance is to have some contact with older, more industrialized, more urbanized, and less provincial parishes than our own. The rural pastor can study the conditions in the city pastorate, the small city pastor can become aware of the stresses in the churches of the huge metropolitan areas, the American pastor can learn the fate of churches in Europe, etc. Another way of developing this farsighted perspective is by listening closely to the troubles of the broken people of our own community. Intensive acquaintance with the pathologies of individuals and groups within our home community gives empirical insight into the shape of things to come for ourselves as well. A scientific way of continuing one's education in the art of anticipation of individual, family, and social dilemmas is the disciplined study of the development of personality in relation to the cultural pattern. At this point the work of the pastor as a prophet and that of the social psychologist and political scientist merge in relevance. The discipline of the pastor in pastoral care and social ethics should have as its cutting edge of purpose the development of the capacity of the pastor to predict and anticipate the troubles of his people. He should not forever be running in the vanguard wondering what has happened, or with little awareness of responsibility for knowing, to some extent at least, what is about to happen. For as Jesus said: "When it is evening, you say, 'It will be fair weather; for the sky is red.' And in the morning, 'It will be stormy today, for the sky is red and threatening.' You know how to interpret the appearance of the sky, but you cannot interpret the signs of the times." (Matt. 16:2-4.) This he said not to prophets but to both the Pharisees and the Sadducees. It is not the will of God that the sons of this world be wiser in their generation than the sons of light. The prophetic pastor does not run when no man pursues, but he has the capacity to anticipate the shape of things to come and the courage to interpret his vision of both the city of man and the City of God to men.

CHAPTER 2

UNDERSTANDING AND COPING
WITH EXTREMISM

THE PASTOR is called to care for people today who are involved on opposing sides of religious, social, and political controversies. His problem of caring for them would be easier if he had a simple, one-faceted relationship to them. The labor organizer, the temperance enthusiast, the civil rights worker, the political ward worker all have one-faceted relationships to their audience: they are single-cause, one-issue people concentrated on labor problems, the liquor problem, civil rights, or the battle for or against this or that political ideology. The pastor, however, has a concern about all these issues plus the general oversight of his people in times of personal crisis such as marriage, the birth of children, the education of children, the draft of young men, the illness of family members, the death of family members, etc.

Furthermore, the pastor is durably related to people and seeks to be their pastor in season and out of season through various social dilemmas that come to crisis in the course of a several-year tenure as pastor.

Yet, in the context of the many-faceted relationships of a pastor to his people, he nevertheless must face, understand, and cope with extremists on religious, social, and political issues. We can learn much about pastoral care by evaluating the pastor's involvement with these extremists.

The extremist can rarely be dealt with apart from a malignant social context. Pastoral care aims at prevention of extremism which, in turn, requires early detection of this social cancer. The purpose of this chapter is to explore the meaning of extremism, identify some of the general characteristics and dynamics of extremists, and to provide the pastor with a discussion pattern for use in two-way communication groups as an " opening " of the understandings of the parish members to tendencies toward extremism in themselves and others.

Extremism can be defined, but to do so is an exercise in spiritual self-examination. Our definitions of extremism are much like outlining our own shadow. They tend to tell others as much about ourselves as they do about extremism. Extremism can be understood, but only by also looking to ourselves lest we too are tempted. Extremism can only be coped with. It cannot be extirpated from the face of the earth.

With this confession of limitation in mind, let me set forth a working hypothesis of extremism. *Extremism is an individual or group reaction against threat.* The sense of threat is out of keeping with reality. Extremism is an overresponse to the stimulus of the threatening agent. Therefore, extremism represents symbolically the distorted and infected personal needs of the extremist. Important human issues and social needs are window dressings of distorted and infected personal problems. The extremist needs to punish and be punished by those whom he opposes. To paraphrase the words of Prov. 28:1, the extremist is one who runs when no one pursues. The more he runs, the farther he gets from the center of things and the heart of the matter.

Yet we cannot lose our own sense of the center of things in reality in saying this. Both you and I have a built-in propensity to think of ourselves as the center and lord of things, both geographically and ideologically. Such a self-evaluation is " this body of death " wrought in the fall of man. This may trap us into thinking that anyone who is at variance with us is an extremist. Hardheaded self-knowledge requires this disclaimer. This realism provides a base for seeing the extremist in terms of his relation or disrelation to the hard core of reality. What do we mean by " reality "? We can use " reality " either psychologically or theologically or both. From a psychological point of view, the hard core of reality is sometimes described as " balance." Thus, the extremist is " unbalanced." At other times, " reality " is psychologically expressed as " appropriateness." Thus, the extremist is spoken of as " inappropriate," and his mood of attack, alarm, and persecution is inappropriate to the situation against which he is reacting. At other times the psychologists use the word " realistic " as opposed to " fantastic." The extremist is thought of as making " fantastic " charges. From a theological point of view, we define reality in terms of the very nature of God and of ourselves as creatures. The extremist can therefore be seen as having measured himself by himself, compared himself with himself, and proved himself not wise. His imagination is a " proud obstacle " that exalts itself against the knowledge of God. Reality is, in opposition to this, the " limits God has apportioned us " (see II Cor. 10:5-17). In theological judgment, the extremist is an idolater; extremism is demonic possession.

Contemporary literature on extremism tends to be written on several different levels of usefulness. The literature of extremists themselves — often calling their opponents extremists — provides case-history material. This literature is useful as examples of extremism. It has objective use such as that which a clock that won't run will give. One has to know what time it is beforehand, even though the clock that won't run is right twice a day! A second kind of literature is found in the attempts of persons involved in such organizations as the Anti-Defamation League of B'nai B'rith to be objective in presenting the facts about extremists. An excellent example of this is Forster and Epstein's *Danger on the Right* (Random House, Inc., 1964). *The New York Times* says that this book is as necessary to the person who is active in civic life as a manual on poisons is to a medicine chest. (*The New York Times Book Review,* October 25, 1964.) However, these books are exposés, not depth studies of the kind of culture and personality that breed extremism. They are not very helpful in learning what to do about the extremist. The third group of books, however, are studies in culture and personality. They help both in understanding and in coping with extremism.

COMMON CHARACTERISTICS OF THE EXTREMIST

Extremists of all varieties have several things in common. Technical literature provides a profile of the extremist. First, the extremist *externalizes* all responsibility and blame. He *projects* blame upon external forces, persons, groups, etc. The psychological mechanism of projection operates overtime in the extremist. Projection is the process whereby one ascribes one's own thoughts, wishes, impulses, inhibitions, and faults to objects and persons in one's environment. The vague, indefinite " they " appears in the stream of conversations, publications, etc. For example, hatred between the races is kept alive and fanned to white heat by industrialists and politicians in order to capitalize on the race issue. Their gain is to maintain control of labor or to secure votes. I saw the deliberate and well-timed use of one Negro as a scapegoat in a political contest where a man campaigning for the United States Senate was beginning to lose the race in a certain county. I saw this, not as a minister, but as a member of a senatorial campaign group when I was a boy of fifteen. The blame for the ills of society during the depression was projected upon the Negro race. In Rome, the Christians were held responsible for hunger and impoverishment created by government corruption. Among churches who channel most of their social concern into fighting the liquor traffic, alcoholics are used as targets for their own projected failures as a people of God. Projection is commonly known as " scapegoating." It is as old as the story of the live goat in Lev. 16:22 which was to " bear all their iniquities upon him to a solitary land."

The second characteristic of the extremist is a rift between the ideas he expresses and the emotions that should normally go with these ideas. For example, stupendous charges and accusations are made with little or no feeling about the person charged and accused. In fact, inappropriate emotions may be there instead. Seemingly honest expressions of personal friendship and affection for the person attacked are claimed. Or the person may act as if nothing had happened personally or emotionally. The rift between ideas and emotions may come in the form of distorted feelings and hostilities about extremely insignificant matters. For example, a lawyer accuses the president of a seminary with misappropriation of funds and distrust of the constituency for having faucet handles that turn off automatically! A mental hygiene society is accused of being actively affiliated with the Communist Party because a Jewish psychiatrist is a part of it! A group of pseudo-intellectuals engage in a cultic vendetta against a denominational executive. They loudly protest that they do not have a better friend than he and that there is nothing personal in their attack. The denominational executive doubts this, but the stark fact about these extremists is that they really do think of him as their friend! Yet there is a profound rift between their intellectual ideas and their emotional affect. This cleavage is deep, unconscious, and irrational. It leads them into a labyrinth of self-justification, ververbalization, and *non sequiturs* of thought, utterance, and action.

As long as the responsible leader moves on the assumption that the ideas and the feelings of extremists are in harmony, he becomes the victim of his own sincerity. He seeks to maintain a consistency between his ideas and his feelings. His religion is often one of strong feelings and practical goodwill. He finds nicely honed logic without appropriate feeling both puzzling and luxurious. Consequently, he is at the mercy of a person who hones his logic and rolls in the luxury of fine distinctions, all the while responding with calculated hardness, suspicion, and ruthlessness. But when the leader responds to the extremist without reference to feeling, and with an eye to a hard-nosed and consistent logic, he finds that the extremist reverts to efforts to please him, placate him, and get on the good side of him. Yet this kind of hard-nosed gamesmanship is alien to our pietistic tradition. Our need to please others, to be in their good graces, and to be nice in our own eyes betrays not only us but the best interests of the extremist himself.

The third characteristic of the extremist is *authoritarianism*. He is what Adorno calls "the authoritarian personality." In a massive and complex tome of research, he and his associates have identified the salient characteristics of the authoritarian personality. (T. W. Adorno *et al., The Authoritarian Personality;* Harper & Brothers, 1950.)

Such a person represses all feelings of weakness and holds weakness in others either with contempt or lack of feeling altogether. He feels that everyone is "out for himself" and that no one basically cares for others. He puts a high premium upon "toughness," which he identifies as "manliness," and rejects tenderness and sympathy as signs of weakness and stupidity. He interprets all relationships in terms of a power struggle, in terms of domination and submission. Cooperation is foreign to him. He distrusts others and avoids obligation or attachment to them. The authoritarian personality is unwilling to accept responsibility for his own acts and habitually avoids taking the initiative. The authoritarian personality has unconscious dependency needs and leans heavily upon the " ones above " him. If he is in a democratic society, he is given to conformity to the group. In an authoritarian society, he depends heavily on the leader. Yet underneath this conformity and submission is a hatred of both the group and the leader. He projects this hostility upon nonconformists to the groups and upon "outsiders" to the "ingroup." These outsiders are often minority groups of other races, nationalities, religious beliefs, and kinds of work.

A consistent cleavage between the seemingly contradictory emotions of tenderness and strength, personal closeness and personal distance, runs through these features of authority. As a pastor deals with extremists, he must remember that direct expressions of kindness are interpreted as signs of stupidity. Attempts to reconcile and reason with the extremist are interpreted as signs of guilt and weakness. The pastor's patience (as he would view it in his own self-image) is interpreted as an invitation to manipulation and exploitation by the extremist. Incident after incident is piled one upon another until the pastor explodes in anger. Then the pastor is accused of being arbitrary, authoritarian, undemocratic, and harsh. All this he is. He has been so protective of his own image of himself as a patient man that he did not challenge directly, firmly, consistently, and without rancor the first infraction of clearly established policy. The first infraction is what the psychologists call the " testing of reality." The pastor is usually new at the task when first infractions occur. He is likely not to challenge then because he is new. The infraction should be challenged on principle and not on the basis of the newness of the man at the job. The pastor who begins a pastorate by running a "tight ship" with clearly defined policies and relationships can later exercise flexibility and warmth. To begin with firmness and later become more flexible is better than to begin with a flabby lack of discipline and be forced to tighten up later. However, this reverses our need to be hail-fellows-well-met.

From the point of view of theological leadership on major social issues, the best approach to the extremist is a preventive one. This can be taken by anticipating controversial issues before they become the occasion for use by extremists as political and economic opportunities to gain money, power, and publicity. When a predictably controversial issue is one to three years in the future, the wise leader will establish a clear policy at once. He states it carefully, dispassionately, and prior to the time when undisciplined men choose up sides. For example, the faculty at the Southern Baptist Theological Seminary established a clear position as to the use of the Revised Standard Version of the Scriptures before the version was published. This document was published widely just prior to the wide circulation of the RSV. The faculty had small-arms fire of extremist criticism, but there was no major conflict. Another theological faculty became involved in a major conflict over the admissions of Negroes *after* the Supreme Court had made a ruling that could have been predicted six years earlier. The schools that have been relatively free of extremist attacks on this issue are those which clearly stated their policy for adequate relationships to Negro students in the late '40s. I am not inferring that advance policy is always possible, nor that it invariably prevents conflict. Rather, I am saying that whenever and wherever prophetic foresight of major issues can work and does, less so-called prophetic arm-waving at the time of extremist conflict is necessary. Less reactive defense is needed. In fact, less extremism takes place. However, the firm maintenance of previously established policy is the price of freedom from the exploitation of weakness by authoritarian personalities, known as extremists, who do arise regardless of what we say or do.

In the fourth place, the extremist is a *cultist*. He must belong to an ingroup. The cult in turn works compulsively at defining the outgroup, the " theys." This cult is uncritical of its group goals, slogans, maxims, clichés, watchwords — its party line. On the other hand, it suspects its individual members, testing and retesting their loyalty. The group in turn is aggressively hostile toward fraternization with anyone who has not been thoroughly indoctrinated and "checked out" as to loyalty. The party line consists of O.K. test words for which members listen. Opposed to the party line are non-O.K. test words with which enemies are identified.

The technical theoreticians about cultic group formations have two helpful concepts. First, August Aichhorn, in his book *Wayward Youth* (Meridian Books, 1955) says that the cultic group is an adolescent phenomenon that comes to pass because of the absence, the ineffectiveness, or the alienation of the adolescents from their real fathers. In our culture, fathers are away from the home most of the time. They are preoccupied and may be weak, nonentities in children's lives when they are at home. They too often are self-absorbed and tyrannical in their unjust domination of their children. The child, therefore, must go outside the home for a substitute for the father. These substitutes are often not forthcoming in the form of adults. The gang becomes the replacement instead. The gang closes in, latches down the hatch, and becomes a self-contained " underground " that recognizes no rules or authority except its own. Any " authority " person, then, *must* be their target. The extremist cults attack specific outstanding leaders and public figures, the real patriarchs of their day. Frank Norris, a hardcore fundamentalist in Dallas during the first part of this century, used this " strange tactic of the extremist " against the patriarch of Southern Baptists, George W. Truett. Like a delinquent gang, the extremists mobilize to punish outstanding leadership for the sins of their own fathers.

Another hypothesis of the extremist cult comes from W. Robertson Smith, namely, that the cult must *offer sacrifice* in order to assuage its own guilt for destroying or attempting to destroy the patriarch or the leader of the masses. The extremist group then chooses a seemingly peripheral or insignificant " totem." For example, theologically, extreme rightist and leftists must have " the resignation " of some more or less defenseless person. He in turn becomes more extreme and *must* be offered up. The political extremist offers up a Walter Jenkins. The Black Muslims offer up a Malcolm X. The insurrectionist group in an institution vows to " get " anyone who fraternizes with the administration. The Judaizers swear neither to eat nor to drink until they have obtained the head of the apostle Paul. In the red-meat leap for power, someone has to be slain and eaten. The extremist group regresses to teen-age atrocity and in-group rituals. To this point, one might call it extremism. But extremism becomes terrorism when the group vendetta regresses even further to primitive or aboriginal blood-thirstiness in its effort to make its point. The Mau Mau has its American counterpart in the Ku-Klux Klan and the American Nazi Party. Such terrorists operate outside the law in much the same way that any other gang does. (For further reading on the points of view set forth here, consult Aichhorn, *Wayward Youth;* and W. Robertson Smith, *The Religion of the Semites,* Meridian Books.)

The fifth characteristic of the extremist is a "didactic stance" of some kind of intellectualism *as an ism.* The extremist is a "gamesman." He plays games with ideas as tools of power in the struggle for dominance. He is only remotely interested in ideas for their own sake, the truth and beauty they afford, or the life they sustain. The extremist may be, therefore, either an anti-intellectual or a pseudo-intellectual. He quotes authorities profusely for his own purpose. That purpose is power, dominance, and mastery at any price in the competitive struggle of things. The anti-intellectual has a reverse English on his didactic stance. He is quick to say, for example, that he is no theologian, but just a common man. Then he takes the theologian to task in order to instruct him perfectly. The pseudo-intellectual, to the contrary, maintains his control by speaking an English that has not yet been spoken by anyone. He rejects his mother tongue. The pseudo-intellectual is often a cultural amputee — cut off from his heritage, with no access to his own personal history. But both the anti-intellectual and the pseudo-intellectual take a didactic stance, build a cult, and keep others out. This group has its own jargon, its own rituals, its own passwords, and its own system of punishment for those who violate the code and ritual of the cult.

The anti-intellectualism and pseudo-intellectualism of the extremist is acutely painful in churches of the free-church tradition which do not require specific educational prerequisites for ordination. In these communions — such as Southern Baptists, the Disciples of Christ, the Society of Friends, etc. — two contrary effects work to spawn extremists of both the anti- and pseudo-intellectual varieties. First, these groups, although they do not require education as a prerequisite to ordination, nevertheless build and support educational institutions. Young people can move from the bottom to the top of the social status system in one generation by the educational route. They pass their parents in educational equipment. They become alienated from their parents. They are rejected by their parents. In order to sustain their own integrity, they must develop an almost fanatical devotion to their teachers and their identity as educated persons. In the process of doing so they may so thoroughly deny their heritage that they themselves become phonies. Their parents may be hurt deeply at losing control over their children through education. Hurt parents may become rabid extremists or prey to extremists who play on their sympathies in order to form a cult of opponents of education and espousers of anti-intellectualism.

In the second place, members of the teaching staffs of colleges and seminaries may be yet in rebellion against their own parental heritages. They become pseudo-intellectuals who further widen the breach between parents and children. Attempts to create better communication between students and parents is only occasionally accepted as a teacher's responsibility. Education, however, should mature lower class young people into responsible, professional persons who can accept their heritage as their own and lay hold of its humble strengths as well as bear the burden of its proud inferiorities.

This, it seems to me, is the responsibility of genuine intellectuals in colleges, universities, and seminaries. Young persons can be taught to appreciate their poverty-ridden and uneducated grandparents and parents who have a face-to-face wisdom learned from life and suffering. At the same time, young people can be introduced to the thought of Plato, Augustine, Kant, Pascal, Schweitzer, Strauss, Rauschenbusch, Freud, Marx, Nietzsche, and a hundred others.

Bad education forces a choice between the two. When his family is uneducated, a young person has real advantage if his teachers are mature and thoroughly educated. To be the victim of half-educated parents and shoddily educated teachers is tragic. Here is where the rub comes. This is where extremism is spawned. The child who comes from the home of a seemingly educated family and is taught in a college or seminary by half-paid, immature, culturally restricted, and partially educated teachers is vulnerable. Extremism is the price we pay for the neglect of quality teaching.

The best antidote to extremism is the development of the genuine intellectuals who can " see life steadily and see it whole." Such teachers make no dichotomy between commitment and the intellectual life. To do so is to set the precondition of extremism at the outset. A genuine intellectual is a committed person. He is not a " smart aleck " filled with the new wine of a few facts. He can go to the edge of the field of human knowledge. Yet he does not lose touch with the tether of that which can be known. He does not lose sight of the center of that which is a known way. He can go to the root of a matter without becoming dry as dust or ignoring the consequences or fruits of his knowledge and commitments. He can mingle with people of other cultures, capture the riches of their wisdom, and not despise or reject the riches and the foundations of his own kinsmen. He can go from Galilee to Judea without his companions' having to wait until he swears before he can be identified as a Galilean. He can go to Jerusalem and contend without rejecting the culture of Tarsus.

The genuine intellectual can be a part of a community without creating a cult as a power lobby in the halls of decision-making bodies. He does not think in " packs " of men who have renounced their humanity in behalf of power, nor is he an organization man who draws his ultimate security from the institution he represents. He can use the symbols of his faith, but he does not mistake them for the substance of his relationship to God. He can use these symbols honestly in terms of their meaning before God. He does not manipulate symbols as ways of getting the best of his neighbor. He can think in abstractions, but he does not take them too seriously. He does not demand that his abstractions become party cries or symbolic slogans in and of themselves. He knows that even the best of abstractions are time-bound. They have their day and then cease to be. The true intellectual knows that the most sophisticated abstraction of today becomes the dead symbol of tomorrow. No symbol is made to replace the knowledge of God as seen in the face of Jesus Christ. This kind of pastor or seminary or college teacher offsets extremism. Such men are hard to come by, but they are the best antidote for extremism.

The extremist, in the sixth place, both victimizes others and is victimized by the propagandistic use of rumor. Gordon Allport developed a theorem and formula for understanding and coping with rumor just after World War II. He says that rumor regularly follows a three-phase pattern of distortion. The first phase he calls " leveling," i.e., omitting from the rumor basic details that are essential for a true understanding of the incident. The extremist systematically omits these details because they negate his preferred interpretation. The second phase of rumor production is " sharpening," i.e., dropping certain details, and thereby sharpening, accentuating, and exaggerating those which are kept. The third phase of the rumor completes it. Allport calls this phase " assimilation." The leveled and sharpened data are now assimilated into the totally different context and mindset of the person who uses the rumor to get his own meaning and to accomplish his own purpose.

Again, Allport reduces rumor production to a predictable formula: $R = i \times a$. The necessary conditions of rumor are (1) the importance of a particular topic, issue, or event and (2) the ambiguity of the evidence about and the statement of the issues at stake. The formula means that " the amount of rumor in circulation will vary with the importance of the subject to the individuals concerned *times* the ambiguity of the evidence pertaining to the topic at issue " (Gordon Allport, *The Psychology of Rumor,* p. 34; Henry Holt & Company, Inc., 1947).

In coping with rumor, therefore, a leader, a pastor, or an executive must pay attention to his own capacity to define the basic issues, to convey adequate information, and to communicate these definitions concisely, thoroughly, and quickly. He cannot wait until extremists begin to do this for him. The reduction of rumor depends upon early communication of full information about important events with a clear and unambiguous definition of what the issues are. When a pastor, a denominational executive, or a teacher is slow, clumsy, indecisive, or timid about giving basic facts and clarifying ambiguity, rumors are generated on the Allport formula of *the importance of the issue multiplied — not added — by the ambiguity created by the tardiness, ineptness, indecision, and timidity of the pastor, executive, or teacher.*

These traits in a leader are, hopefully, not due to laziness, inability, or cowardice on the part of pastors, executives, and teachers. They are due to a misunderstanding of kindness, a fear of hurting opponents and critics or of seeing themselves as somehow unchristian if they lay the facts and issues clearly before their constituency. The extremist gambles on this pietism. He usually wins by intimidating the pastor into keeping what he knows and thinks to himself. Then the pastor becomes the victim of his own kindness.

The extremist interprets this generosity as an admission of guilt or a sign of weakness, and his "group" moves in for the kill. I hope I am not being unfaithful to the words of our Lord when I say that he must have meant this when he said: "Behold, I send you out as sheep in the midst of wolves; so be wise as serpents and innocent as doves" (Matt. 10:16). The pietistic leader is as a sheep in the midst of wolves in the face of the rapacity of the extremist.

The extremist is, in the seventh place, characterized by *commercialism;* that is, his need for luxury and the symbols of affluence tend to motivate his crusading impulses. Only occasionally is the rake-off motive absent from extremism. Among the anti-intellectuals this takes the crasser form of money and goods. Among the pseudo-intellectuals this takes a more refined form of time off with pay from institutions which they criticize. The commercialism of the extreme rightists in this country is estimated to be a multimillion-dollar business. An example of this concerns the money-raising results of a variety of schemes used to extract money from the public through pseudoreligious, pseudopatriotic, and pseudopolitical facades. On the other side of radical left extremism, money-getting tends to take the form of so-called research grants that never result in tangible reports of honest work done. The "foundation tramp" is a familiar face on university campuses. The hidden agenda of commercialism, however carefully waxed in, nevertheless, is the hallmark of the extremist. The extremist tends to love luxury, avoid work, and survive parasitically on the labors of others.

Some Hypotheses as to the Dynamics of Extremism

Several composite working hypotheses prove helpful in understanding the underlying motivation and/or dynamics of the behavioral characteristics of extremism. First, the sheer success of the extremist with masses of people is explained by Erich Fromm in his *Escape from Freedom* (Farrar & Rinehart, Inc., 1941) in the following way. Children are brought up in homes where they are taught by parents that the parent can do no wrong, no matter how harsh or unjust they in fact may be. The cardinal virtue is obedience to parents who, for all practical purposes, take the place of God. The child grows to adulthood as a basically dependent and weak person who relinquishes his personal initiative and gains strength by submitting to a supposedly "wise and powerful" leader. Thus, he escapes from freedom at the price of his own individuality. On the other hand, Adorno's theory complements this with the authoritarian leader who has nothing but contempt for the weak, imperializes the indecisive, and conquers the opposition by dividing them. He in turn is the product of a home where parents were alternately harsh and overindulgent in their care of the child. They punished him roundly, but, when he got into trouble outside the home, they overprotected him and never let him learn from his own experience. He respects no authority except his own. In other words, he is a law unto himself and all the rest of the world is wrong and to blame. This he learned from his youth up. He makes a real extremist because he is the product of alternating extremes of hot and cold parental treatment.

A second hypothesis concerning the extremist is the hypothesis of paranoia. The paranoiac has a fixed system of carefully wedged in ideas. He is coldly persuasive with the ideas. The ideas are convincing and subtle. They are incomplete, and, as in rumor, necessary elements of reality and fact have been carefully deleted. This partial and cunning system serves as a major presupposition of his thought. Once a person has accepted his major presupposition, all else is as logical as can be. The flaw lies in the presupposition.

For example, here is a presupposition: " The Sunday School Board *is* just *a publishing house* to *circulate* the liberal *ideas* of those atheistic *seminary professors*." If you accept the total presupposition, and you cannot totally deny it, you are hooked by the extremist. If you are a dependent, weak person, you are likely to be overpowered. If you are strong enough to resist, you are wrong enough to be suspected. On the other hand, the presupposition has a partial measure of the truth in it. The Sunday School Board *is* a publishing house! It *does* circulate the ideas of seminary professors! The extremist's statement is a half-truth. The truth in the statement then is inflamed by accusations of deviousness, persecution, and character attack.

This attack is the second feature of the paranoiac — i.e., of persecution, or that a sinister plot is being perpetrated by evil men. The third feature of paranoia is grandiosity or delusions of grandeur. If the extremist is permitted to " take over," then all that is wrong will be set right. A messianic take-over will restore Israel to the " good old days." But all these characteristics buttress the main feature of paranoia — the fear of body contact or personal closeness. Any attempt, therefore, at reconciliation is a panic-stricken threat to the extremist. This is the hidden agenda of his cold-bloodedness, insensitivity, sadistic humor, and defiance of good men's attempts to be kind to him. A comparative respect for this fear of closeness must be built into our approach to the extremist, for he will not be changed in this respect. A chilly realism on the leaders' part will compensate for it much as insulin offsets diabetes but does not cure it.

A third explanation of the causes of extremism can be based upon W. H. Whyte's thesis of the organization man. He asks for an individualism *within* organization life. The extremist, from this point of view, then, is the man who fictitiously assumes that he can be free of the organization by rebelling against it, fighting it, and seeking to destroy it. Whyte's thesis is that if a person does this, he simply moves to another organization or starts one of his own, thus becoming all that he fought. Whyte says that attacks on organizations are usually because of the evils of the organization. The real damage done by the organization, however, is more subtle; it is the beneficence and paternalism that takes away initiative in behalf of security. In this roots the sense of luxury, the will to power, and the parasitism of the archextremist who commercializes his cause, be it evangelism, counseling, anticommunism, or what. He is looking for security, not leadership and creative social change. On the other hand, the leader, the teacher, the executive in an organization, may depend heavily on the bureaucracy for the same motive of security. Thus he fails to exercise prophetic anticipation and leadership that outdistances the extremist attack. He does not define, inform, and remove ambiguity from the issues. He depends upon endless meetings of committees, subcommittees, and boards for this. The resulting confusion becomes grist for the extremist's mill.

The hard-gained teamwork of effective organization cannot be forsaken by a leader taking too much responsibility and not consulting his fellow responsibility bearers. The days of the tycoon leader and prima donna are either over or numbered, and we are in an industrial and technologically organized society. Nevertheless, Whyte's thesis is that we need to reactivate the principle of the individual leadership as a corrective of our conformism to the organization itself. I would add further that without this sense of leadership on the part of those in authority we may expect the kind of usurpation of leadership evident in extremism. (See William H. Whyte, Jr., *The Organization Man;* Simon and Schuster, Inc., 1956.)

Two-Way Communication About Extremism

The false prophecies of extremism call for "beating one's opponent down" — either verbally or otherwise. This rules out listening to him. True prophets conduct — as did Jeremiah — listening-in campaigns. One of the most effective ways of dealing with extremism, therefore, is to create group sessions in which two-way communication — both listening and speaking, both being heard and hearing — can take place.

The pastor cannot farm out this responsibility to other people. Although he can involve other leaders in helping him to carry this responsibility, he himself must activate his work as a teacher. New groups for this purpose are rarely necessary in a church. There are enough dead, inactive, or limping organizations in the church that the pastor can bring vack to vitality and use. In fact, purposeless and meaningless groups in a church are often used by extremists themselves in order to propagate their cause.

In dealing with the problems of extremism, I have not named any particular group as extremists, as you will notice in the previous sections of this chapter. The reason for this is threefold: First, to avoid the pitfall of the extremist himself when he resorts to name-calling. This is not communication; it is a substitute for profanity. Second, to provide a basis for self-examination whereby a reader or a listener may judge for himself as to whether he and/or his neighbors are extremists. Third, to leave an open end to the discussion that invites dialogue and conversation and not merely an emotional reaction.

One person responded to a public discussion of the material in this chapter with a letter. She asked to *which* group of extremists was I referring and named several kinds from her own personal acquaintances. I replied by saying that I had deliberately not named anyone or any group for the above reasons and in order to get my audience to think for themselves rather than merely to conform to my authority or to rebel against it. Instead of resenting this approach, my correspondent answered me with a reflective letter in which she revealed her own struggles of decision and concluded by saying, " If your objective was to help me think for my-self, you have accomplished it."

With such a mood in mind, a pastor can begin to be an effective group discussion leader. The problems of extrem-ism are individual in origin but express themselves at the small-group level. The pastor can best deal with them at the small-group level. There will be feedback from the group into individual counseling and major positive suggestions for preaching at the congregational level. But adult discus-sion groups provide the best instrument for pastoral care of the problems of extremism. These cannot be lecture ses-sions, although the use of such research data and hypotheses as have been presented in this chapter can be effective either as reading matter for such groups or as a basis for opening presentations to a group. In either event, the purpose of the reading or the presentation would be just that — to open two-way communication.

The Lord told the prophet Ezekiel to stand upon his feet that he might speak *with* him. The pastor can no longer use his role as pastor as a privileged sanctuary from which to hand down directives in an authoritarian didactic stance of his own to dependent people — even against extremism. Both he and they must learn to converse with each other. The pastor must — under God — create a ground upon which he can say to his people: " Stand upon your feet, and I will speak *with* you."

CHAPTER 3

PASTORAL COUNSELING AND THE RACIAL DILEMMA

A DILEMMA presents an antagonist with two or more alternatives (or " horns "). Each is equally conclusive against him, whichever he chooses. It is a choice between unsatisfactory alternatives. As Jonathan Swift says:

> A strong dilemma in a desperate case!
> To act with infamy, or quit the place.

The above definition of a dilemma is found in Webster's Unabridged Dictionary. It describes the " thrown situation " of a pastor in a community where the race problem is more than an academic discussion of clearly stated absolutes. Here the race issue involves the face-to-face relationships of people of sharply differing attitudes and vested interests. The pastor is likely to be gored by either horn of the dilemma.

As I begin the discussion, therefore, of the topic " Pastoral Counseling and the Racial Dilemma," I return to the theme of the ambiguity and uncertainty that attends the work of the pastor in a community where racial tension is either chronic or acute. In order to clarify some — not all — of this ambiguity and uncertainty at the outset, I must do two things: (1) show the difference between itinerant and resident pastors, and (2) clarify something of the burden and witness of being a Southern pastor.

Resident Versus Itinerant Ministries

First, I must call attention to two kinds of pastors, both of whom serve important functions in relation to the race problems and other problems of our day. Their functions, however, are drastically different. One kind of pastor is the resident, institutional pastor of a local church. He must deal with *all* the problems of his church and community all the time. He cannot — ordinarily — restrict his ministry to *one* problem such as the race problem, women's voting rights, the liquor problem, or, for that matter, the problem of mental health, etc. The resident pastor must cope with each of these simultaneously in a variety of ways. He cannot, however, become a " single issue " exponent of the Christian faith to the exclusion of all other issues.

Furthermore, in seminary, as Dr. Jesse Ziegler of the American Association of Theological Schools has said, the pastor was educated to think of the church as a world fellowship of unhindered love of men as neighbors and love for God. But in practice, the church is an institution with traditions, a set of ruling families, and with a specific cultural pattern that it holds dearer than the Bible itself. The resident minister is, to use a military figure, like the commanding officer of an occupation army. He is assigned to " keep the peace," to maintain a semblance of order, and to keep the native population reasonably quiet if not happy.

The second kind of minister is the itinerant, nonresident, roving minister. He usually is a " single issue " minister. He may devote himself entirely to evangelism, leaving the care of new converts to the resident pastor. He may be a temperance worker, concentrating entirely on the problem of the liquor traffic. The care of alcoholics and their families he leaves to the resident pastor. He may be a " mental health expert " whose single concern is the problems of religion and mental health. He, too, often leaves the care of the mentally ill to the local pastor. (For a roving minister to become so " classified " as to preach a series of exegetical sermons on The Book of Jeremiah or The Letter of James, therefore, shatters the pattern. For that matter, for him to preach at all comes as a surprise to many.) Or an itinerant minister may be a " race relations " man. At the particular time in history when the " special " single issue of these persons becomes "hot," they are controversial figures to the nth degree. They are either idolized or defamed, but few are indifferent to them.

This is not the first time in history that gaping chasms of difference have appeared between these two kinds of ministers. The Rechabites and Nazirites did not drink wine, but it was not a rejection of wine, as such, that caused this. The wine represented the shift of the Jews from a nomadic, itinerant, unrooted group of shepherds to a settled, agricultural, resident crowd of vinedressers! The voices crying in the wilderness were people who lived on locusts and honey. They did not belong to the establishment.

The roving, itinerant, unrooted minister is more like, militarily speaking, the Marines. He campaigns. He " hits the beachheads." He is likely to be thought of as atrocious as well as ferocious. He does not deal in niceties. He has only one objective in mind: combat and victory. He aims to overcome. It does not do to televise him in action; he is not too careful when it comes to women and children!

But the commercial and publicity values attached to the functions of both the resident pastor and the itinerant crusader today blur the almost too easy distinction drawn here. The basic sociological differences are clear, but to make a hero of one and a villain of either is to edit out the element of human cussedness that can make both a hero and a villain out of both of them either alternately or simultaneously. For example, neither is by the nature of the case exempt from the love of money. The corruption of evangelism at this point, for example, is the handwriting on the wall for the itinerant " mental health " preachers and " civil rights workers " of today. The love of luxury is no respecter of causes. If we took the profit motive out of both evangelism and the liquor industry, we would probably have less of both, but what we did have would be of much better quality! More simplicity in both the resident and the itinerant minister's mode of life would bring them closer together. When people go looking for a prophet, they do not look for one clothed in soft raiment, gorgeously appareled, living in luxury in kings' houses. (Luke 7:25.)

The Burden and Witness of a Southern Pastor on the Race Issue

As a Southerner, I must say that no discussion of pastoral care and the race issue would be complete without a frank admission on my part of a personal ambivalence which fills any conscientious Southern pastor who seeks to be honest with himself and others about the race issue. Ambiguity is built into the very being of a Southern pastor on this issue. The louder he proclaims his certainties, the more ambiguous he becomes. I have chosen to call this built-in ambivalence the burden and the witness of the Southern pastor. At this point, I am being deliberately autobiographical without apology.

The Burden. The plight of the Negro in the South has not been his alone to bear. The poor white has shared this tragedy in his own way as well. I grew up in the cotton-mill ghettos of South Carolina. These cotton mills were built near enough to the city to be by a railroad. They were far enough away that the people were neither a part of the city nor a part of the rural area. They were industrial ghettos. These ghettos were built on the social infection of the tenant-farmer system. This was the cotton plantation owners' ugly alternative to Negro slavery. The ignorant and the dispossessed white shared the same fate as the Negro. These ghettos were built on the practice of child labor. Little children under the age of ten would go to work on Monday morning before daylight and would not see daylight except through the windows of the mill until Sunday morning. These ghettos were built upon the use of "tokens" for currency at that social scab known as "the company store." Here the substitutes for currency could be spent; they could not be spent elsewhere. Laborers, living on incomes too small to support their families, would borrow on unearned pay against the future. Within a month or two, they would be in total debt and their whole income would be returned to them in company script. Script could be sold to various and vague individuals for eighty cents on the dollar to get Federal currency. This script could be spent only at the company store. Therefore, like the man in Tennessee Ernie Ford's song, they couldn't die because they were in debt to the company store!

More recently these practices of child labor and company-store enslavement have been discontinued. However, the short-term loan company has replaced both systems. In my hometown of Greenville, South Carolina, I stood recently on the main street of the town and could count thirteen short-term loan companies within eyesight without having to move my position.

A further example of the burden I feel as a Southern

pastor is my awareness of the way in which poor whites have been pitted against poor Negroes in the South in order to maintain the aristocracy of the few and the servility of the many. Poor white has been deliberately set against poor Negro to the benefit of the rich white. This has been true in both the industrial and the rural areas. In the meantime, absentee ownership of both mill and farm has allowed the owners to live in the cities, towns, and villages while the laborers lived on the farm and in the cotton-mill village.

The great burden of this social system grew up as a reaction against pre-Civil War slavery which had been outlawed. As one Negro leader has said:

> If it may be said of the slavery era that the white man took the world and gave the Negro Jesus; then it may be said of the Reconstruction Era that the Southern Aristocracy took the world and gave the poor white man Jim Crow. He gave him Jim Crow — and when his wrinkled stomach cried out for the food that his empty pockets could not provide, he ate Jim Crow — a psychological bird that told him that no matter how bad off he was, at least he was a white man — better than black men. He ate Jim Crow, and when his undernourished children cried out for the necessities that his low wages could not provide he showed them the Jim Crow signs on the busses and in the stores, on the streets and in the public buildings — and his children too learned to feed upon Jim Crow, their last outpost to psychological oblivion.
>
> Thus, the threat of the free exercise of the ballot by the Negro and white masses alike resulted in the establishment of a segregated society. They *segregated* southern money from the *poor whites,* they segregated *southern poor* from the *rich whites,* they segregated southern churches from Christianity; they segregated *southern minds* from honest thinking, and they segregated the Negro from everything. (Martin Luther King, Jr., " Mont-

gomery March No Accident," *Southern Christian Leadership Conference Newsletter,* Vol. 11, No. 10 [April–May], pp. 9–10.)

The church has been used in this system as an arena for the exercise of leadership among the poor. The ministry as a profession was the one gateway to social improvement. Therefore, little wonder is it that the poor white, no matter how well-to-do he has become, and the poor Negro, no matter how desperate his plight, both tend to want to hang on to the leadership of their churches. The church becomes the only vestige of identity either has, regardless of how limited the world view of that church may be. He is not about to give it up. The owners of farm and mill, however, have through the years of my life seen the church as a way of keeping the natives — both white and colored — from becoming restless. Perhaps the church has too often been the instrument whereby oppressors have oppressed the oppressed. This is the burden which I bear as a Southern pastor. Southern pastors have been involved in this nefarious system and have been too uncritical and too dependent upon the system to raise a voice of resistance.

The Witness. However, out of the small churches of mill and farm in the South has come a witness. There has come a witness of rugged individualism of a conversion theology. This individualism tends to deify personal will. It inbreeds a feeling of destiny in spite of the clutch of fate. I recall vividly a woman who lived near us when I was a five-year-old boy. She sang camp-meeting gospel songs while she cooked for her family. I was not in school. I was the youngest and as a preschooler I would visit around her kitchen and as she sat on the porch preparing food for cooking. I recall very well one occasion on which she said to me that she and her whole family were bound to the mill for life.

But she said: " You can be different. God has a purpose for you. Find it! " I have never forgotten this. The poignancy of her awareness of being in bondage to a system nevertheless was offset by a feeling of destiny in spite of the clutch of the fate of the system.

Eleven years later in a cotton-mill Baptist church in Greenville, South Carolina, I was confronted by a pastor's wife with the claims of Jesus Christ upon my life. I committed my life to Jesus Christ. I was led to believe and have never had reason to doubt basically the cause of what happened through the encounter with Jesus Christ. I could by the power of God rise above the determining power of that system. I was in bondage, not only to my personal sins, but to the sins of society upon us. The redemption I experienced in Jesus Christ created a new forgiveness of my sins and a measure of forgiveness on my part of those who had sinned against me. This gave me a beachhead of freedom that has never been removed from me.

Therefore, I as a Southern pastor have both a burden to bear and a witness to proclaim. It is inevitable that I shall all my days have, therefore, an ambivalence about being a Southerner. On the one hand, I feel that we sit idly in the presence of the great bondage of people of the land and often use our commitment to a segmented " specialty " called religion as an opiate to ease the pain of the bondage. On the other hand, I thank God for the rugged individualism of conversion theology that inbred in me a feeling of destiny in spite of the clutch of fate.

Professionally speaking, I have little or no right to speak in terms of technical data as a " specialist in race relations." However, I may have a point of view with which to talk with you in terms of my own professional discipline as a pastoral counselor, as a professor of pastoral care, and as one who takes seriously the social as well as the personal level.

I have for twenty-three years been involved in the processes of social change that are aimed at changing the function of the Christian pastor from that of an itinerant, unrooted, and untrained person to that of a rooted, disciplined, caring pastor. We have, in the field of pastoral care, sought to establish pastors as more than mere traveling public speakers and entertainers and, at the same time, something other than the keeper of the bees for an institutional church that does not want to be stung.

Furthermore, the ultimate issues of social ethics are the emergency demands laid upon the practicing pastoral counselor. We grapple tactically with the problems of the unskilled laborer — black or white — and the relationship of his lack of skill to family instability. Therefore, the necessity of a strategic knowledge of social change, social class, and social ethics for the effective pastoral counselor goes without saying. Pastoral counseling cannot be done on a purely individual basis in such a way as to avoid the great evils of the world. We are in great danger among pastoral counselors of making the same mistake that the nineteenth-century evangelist made: the mistake of snatching individual persons from the fires of social evil and never taking any responsibility for the proclamation of the gospel concerning the social evils themselves. As Alan Paton has said in his poignant book *Cry, the Beloved Country,* " the counselors of our land have counsel for many things except for the main thing: the brokenness of the people as a people."

In the face of this brokenness over the problem of race, we need now to deal with the function of a pastor amid racial tension.

The Function of the Resident Pastor
Amid Racial Conflict

Deliberate choice is made here to discuss pastoral care amid race conflict in terms of the resident pastor and not in terms of the itinerant civil rights worker. We are not thinking here even in terms of the resident pastor teacher who moves into a racially tense community from somewhere else. When the "heat is on," so to speak, he is present but moves out when the open conflict and public attention is drawn somewhere else. The resident pastor has to live with the situation day in and day out. When asked why he did or did not do something dramatic in a race conflict, all his other excuses are unconvincing as compared with the unnoticed statement of a few: " We have to live here." These pastors' children are members of the student bodies of schools that are being desegregated. These pastors register to vote in the same places where voter registration is the issue. Their names are in the telephone books, and their homes are accessible to anonymous telephone calls and to bomb threats and attempts. Their livelihood depends upon their relationship to a local congregation.

Already the (listener) reader begins to shuffle restlessly. He or she begins to say to himself or herself: " A case is being made now to exonerate the resident pastor from any responsibility in race conflicts." If this is so, I would answer: " Steady yourself a bit and wait. All I am doing here is to encourage empathy on your part for the resident pastor. His situation must be understood if it is to be changed and strengthened."

Such understanding must include a hypothesis that *given two ministers with the same or similar convictions on racial opportunity and justice, the motives and methods of the one who is a resident pastor will be vastly different from the motives and methods of the itinerant civil rights worker or visiting pastor from another community in effecting those same convictions.* If this hypothesis is true, what is some of the supporting evidence?

First, the resident pastor represents an institution, a local church, and a multiplicity of causes. The civil rights worker represents no institution and only one cause.

Second, the resident pastor is in face-to-face, private communication with the power structure, or leadership, of his own institution. His methods are privacy and persuasion, not publicity and coercion. When he does use publicity or personal power, he must carefully weigh its long-term as well as its short-term results. In other words, he must " weigh in " before he starts " throwing his weight around."

Third, the resident pastor is accused of " guilt by association " in the attacks made upon him by the public press and by his fellow ministers who are interested in but do not live with the community undergoing a racial revolution. Conversely, the local leadership of his church is likely to define his duties very sharply and as having nothing to do with such problems as " mental health," " family troubles," and " race problems."

One incident of this attitude just described stands out in my memory as the pastor of an old, established church. I had been active in efforts to establish a marriage counseling service in our city. The story of our committee's work was in the newspaper on a Saturday. On Sunday I was to preach on the nature of true worship. The fourth chapter of the Fourth Gospel — in which Jesus discusses worship with a Samaritan woman he knew to have had five husbands — was the text. Just before the service, I was buttonholed by the president of the local public transit company. He told me that he was not pleased with the article in Saturday's paper and did not think it the place of a pastor to be meddling in people's "marriage troubles." The place of the pastor was to preach the gospel and win souls to Christ. This, to him, was the purpose of the church and its ministry.

It would have been easy to have smoothed things over privately with this man and to have lambasted him and his kind from the pulpit. The text I had chosen already gave me a perfect launching pad for putting such an attack into orbit. It would have vented my hostility, and I would have "gotten it off my chest" in a public heroism.

Instead, I decided to deal with him privately as he had chosen to do with me. I explained to him that I appreciated his being concerned about what his pastor did and said. I told him I felt that people's marriage conflicts were inseparable from their redemption as whole persons before God. I told him that I did not agree with his understanding of the gospel as being separated from people's troubles at home, but that my disagreement had nothing to do with my friendship for him or my full intention to minister to him and his family as their pastor if and when they should need me.

This happened eighteen years ago, and yet it comes nostalgically back to me as I read these words on the race problem from a letter dated October 8, 1965, from a young pastor in a large church in a city which has been torn asunder with race conflict:

> The experiences which my wife and I have had here have been very helpful to us. We have come to appreciate what it means to stick to being a Christian. It is not easy to make glib statements about things when we see how much people stand to lose, or at least they think they do. There are ministers and some people who feel that the churches should have a voice in the Negroes' struggle.

The most frequently mentioned reason for our keeping silent goes something like this: "We do not want to hurt our primary concerns — winning people to Christ, teaching them to grow, spreading the gospel." I am afraid that unless we deal with this problem we will cast a shadow of doubt upon the validity of our primary concerns. We ask you to pray that all may find God's way of leading people to do what they suspect they should do.

Herein lies the dilemma of the resident pastor on the race issue, told more eloquently by this former student of mine than I can tell it. What, then, are some guidelines for the pastoral care of a local community by a resident pastor in the face of this issue?

Preaching, Pastoral Care, and Racial Problems

The task of preaching can neither be separated from nor equated with the total pastoral responsibility of a minister on a given issue. As has been indicated before, the temptation of the person who focuses his concerns in pastoral care is to separate it from preaching and from dealing with great social issues en masse. From this point of view, a discussion of pastoral care would be limited entirely to such matters as counseling with individual Negroes and their families, dealing with social casework problems of the deprived and multiproblem family, both Negro and white, etc. On the other hand, the problem of dealing with the race question is often *equated* with his function as a preacher. If he is not preaching on it from the pulpit, this means that he is silent and doing nothing. As another pastor in a racially torn city wrote me:

Just because we do not lambast someone from the pulpit, we are said to be silent. We get no public or private praise for endless hours of telephoning, conferring pri-

vately with the principal contenders, and trying to get
some common ground upon which all men can stand
upon and at least talk with each other.

But preaching itself cannot be ruled out in behalf of a
purely private, invisible ministry. Both the content and the
methodology of preaching on controversial issues can be informed by what we know about pastoral care. At this point,
several things need to be said.

Preaching can explore and expose the background, the
fallacy, and the measure of truth in the statement that involvement in any social issue will " hurt our primary concerns — winning people to Christ, teaching them to grow,
spreading the gospel." Where did this idea come from?
Southerners were heavily involved in a great social issue —
slavery. They suffered a humiliating and demoralizing de-
feat. Southerners withdrew from all political and social issues except prohibition and the separation of church and
state. More recently they have added " states' rights " some-
what surreptitiously. Beyond this they have felt that politics
and religion must not be mixed. This philosophy is under-
girded by a nineteenth-century political philosophy and
concept of evangelism. This philosophy and evangelism
magnify as divine the rights of the individual, atomize personality into mental, physical, and spiritual categories un-
related to one another. When we compound this with a
denomination's primary objective to survive and outdo
other denominations, we have some inkling of where the
laissez-faire attitude toward any problem but that of gain-
ing converts arose.

The fallacy of this can be offset by a reaffirmation of the
Biblical understanding of the wholeness of man. He is a
totality both individually and corporately. The separation
of the gospel from all the concerns of man is Biblically rep-

rehensible. The people attempted this separation when they demanded that Aaron make a golden calf, and they said: "These are your gods, O Israel. . . . ! " (Ex. 32:4). Jesus tied all of life into a unity when he conferred with a racially different (Samaritan), sexually different (woman) person about the nature of his own identity (as the Christ) and the meaning of the worship of God. Race is simply *one* of the many issues declared off limits by this nineteenth-century kind of philosophy and evangelism.

However, the measure of truth in the insistence upon "our primary concerns" as over against the "race issue" is to be affirmed as well. No *one* issue subsumes the totality of the gospel. The race issue is no exception. The family itself cannot become the center of the gospel. Otherwise, we wind up with a set of hearthstone gods and not the totality of the gospel. The race issue is not the heart of the gospel of Jesus Christ, even though it may be the present festering point in the broken and bleeding body of Christ. Already the issue of war with Orientals begins to draw both Negroes and whites to mingle their blood on the battlefields of Vietnam. To make any *one* issue the central, lasting issue of the warfare of Jesus Christ is in itself a kind of idolatry. The sin of a segregated society lies right here: it forces a Negro to plan his whole existence around this one thing — his race. It leaves him no diversity of choice among the many issues of the Christian at work in the world.

The methodology of preaching on the race issue — or on any controversial issue — is as important as the content. Present-day preaching methods do not make possible a fair relationship for dealing with controversy. It is inappropriate to the point of being grounds for charges of "disturbing the peace" or "mental incompetency" to interrupt a preacher to ask a question or to make a comment. We have learned in pastoral care that the preacher needs to " listen " in counseling and not just to " speak " as in preaching. More recently we are learning that in both counseling and preaching he needs to listen and to speak in genuine dialogue. How can this be done in preaching? There are several ways.

The preacher can anticipate great social issues long before they become " hot " with controversy. He can establish two-way communication discussion groups in which people can reflect together over the facts and feelings involved. After the Los Angeles riots, for example, a wise pastor would discuss the question as to the causes and prevention of such riots in his city. Varieties of opinions could be expressed without rigid " positions " becoming battlegrounds.

Another pastor who preaches forthrightly on the race issue discusses the subject and his material with his deacons and other lay leaders before preaching. He gets their objections beforehand and answers them honestly on a face-to-face basis. They may continue to disagree with him, but they do not feel they have had "no say " or have been trapped with no opportunity to " answer back."

Another pastor has feedback sessions after a sermon in which persons who want to can " answer back " and tell him " how they heard him." This is a real test of a pastor's being open to criticism, but it is a creative opening for him to learn from his laymen. This particular pastor feels keenly that laymen themselves should have the opportunity to speak on occasions other than Laymen's Sunday. He asks: " Why should all the preaching be done by one man when many may have burning witnesses to bear? "

Another pastor chose a different method of getting audience participation on the race issue. On one Sunday he referred to the racial revolution:

A new day is coming. No force under heaven can halt the march of that new day. No power or force can resist the force of an idea. This is an idea. The hour has come. The old ark is "amoverin'," and we'd better be wise to let it move. Or we'll subject ourselves to terrible agony, and still have it move anyway. . . . I don't know how to crusade . . . but I will do whatever it costs to lend my voice to what seems right [in race relations] with sanity in my posture and attitude as God gives me strength. Our church has never taken open action on the question of admitting Negroes. I have always felt that there was no need to do so, for there never has been any closing action on this question. I have said from this pulpit, with people of other races present — " whoever you are, you are welcome as a worshiper at this church if worship is your purpose. I want the membership to hear me on this. During the coming week, I want your reactions. If you think my assumption that our membership is open to all believers and worshipers of Jesus Christ is wrong, I expect you to say so. If it is right, I expect you to say so."

During the succeeding week, this sermon drew into the pastor's study, into telephone conversation, and into casual street and shop contact many who had varied opinions and reactions. He established face-to-face contact with three extremists, one to the left and two to the right. He was able to carry the major leadership of the congregation with his statement of policy because of long-established trust and previous dialogue with them as a group and as individuals.

ADMINISTRATIVE LEADERSHIP AND RACIAL TENSION

The administrative role of a pastor likewise cannot be disentangled from the role of a caring pastor in times of racial tensions. The case example of a pastor-administrator in the August, 1965, issue of *The Baptist Program* is one of the few case records of a church facing the problem of Negroes in a Baptist church in Georgia seeking to be seated for worship. In July, 1964, the deacons had established a temporary policy to seat the Negroes if they came. One deacon voted against it, the policy was not announced to the church, and the deacons assumed that the church " would go along, at least for a while, with whatever decision they made."

The problem erupted into open conflict when a Negro actually attended. The deacons were accused of treachery and trying to run the church. Every deacon was telephoned by two men and was "blessed out." The pastor felt that the major mistake was the breakdown of communication between deacons and congregation. A church vote was taken. The church had 625 resident members. Less than half the resident members voted. By a majority of 150 to 95, a vote was taken *not* to seat Negroes, even though the pastor preached strongly in favor of seating the Negroes.

The pastor of this church was grieved as much by this as he had been the day his father died. No one wants to " run him off," but he is apathetic. His problem is whether he wants to stay or not. He concludes with the question: " What use is there in preaching in such a situation? "

Administratively speaking, the pastor can, with foreknowledge, discuss this whole matter with the leadership of a church before and as he becomes their pastor. He can enter a clear covenant with them as to their action in such crises. Many churches demand this of the pastor — that he will support their " stand." Many pastors refuse to become pastors of a church that demand conformity to segregation. A few pastors, much sought after, have entered a covenant that such a crisis would be met by simply seating all worshipers regardless of race. When the leadership of one church reversed the covenant they had with the pastor, and voted to refuse Negroes a place to worship, he simply resigned on the spot. He reminded them that they had broken their word with him. They reversed their position in order to keep their word.

I record these instances in an anecdotal manner. Careful church historians would do well to use the clinical method and record the living human documents of churches in action facing racial crises. The clinical method is not new, nor was it original with pastoral care and counseling folk. It is as old as the Bible itself and has simply fallen into disuse amid theologians' declarations of hot certainties.

PASTORAL COUNSELING AND RACIAL TENSION

I am concluding this chapter where many would have expected me to begin it. As a clinician in pastoral counseling, I do not believe there is a separate procedure for dealing with counseling difficulties of which the race issue is a part. I base this on the assumption of the personhood of the Negro and the white, just as in the succeeding chapter I assume the personhood of man and woman.

As a pastoral counselor, therefore, to me the poignancy of the race problem is akin to and not basically different from the still sadness that comes to me from other types of situations. Occasionally someone tells me that as a seminary professor I am out of touch with the masses. But I think that any person who has a regular job, a home of his own, eats three meals a day, is on a diet, has a college education, and is able to give his children what they need is likely to be "out of touch with the masses." The Los Angeles riots of 1965 underscore the "out-of-touchness" with the masses of even the emerging middle-class Negro leader (*Newsweek*, August 30, 1965, p. 19).

But through pastoral counseling I have been able to get

back in touch occasionally with those masses. I have counseled with Negro mothers whose husbands have no skill wherewith to keep a steady job. I have counseled with white girls who were taught by their Southern mothers to have nothing to do with a Negro playmate after they reached puberty. I have sensed their grief and lack of understanding. I have counseled with Negro students — boys — who live in mortal fear of being accused of social aggressiveness toward a white girl. I have counseled with bankers in interceding for a young Negro schoolteacher to be allowed a loan on a house. I have seen his house stand unfinished because it was located in a Negro ghetto. He was expected to live in a shack like all the others even though his money was as certain as that of a white man. I have worked with social caseworkers to find an adoptive home for the child of an unwed mother whose lover — not a rapist — was a Negro boy. I have had these and other similar experiences as a pastoral counselor.

However, I believe that the minister as a pastoral counselor has the following tasks to accomplish when he is fortunate enough to establish counseling contact with the Negro of today and tomorrow:

1. Encourage him toward an identity of his own. This must not be a negative identity of the kind that G. Mansfield Collins, pastor of the All Saints Community Church in Watts, Los Angeles, speaks: " Tonight [the unemployed Negro] is somebody. Tonight he has an identity." This identity must not be a derived identity, by reason of his becoming *like* the white man. I told a young Negro pastor in my community when he asked me to lead a workshop on pastoral care: " No, you have excellent training yourself. I will attend, take careful notes, study along with you, but you lead the workshop and get some of your own leaders

to lead with you. Then I will tell you what you have taught me that as a white man I did not know." This we did, and they discovered a leadership that was uniquely theirs in which I could share and from which I could learn.

2. Introduce individual Negro men to a new role as men who can provide for and stay with the families they start. In 1960, according to a recent study, 21 percent of Negro families were headed by the mother as compared with 18 percent in 1950 and with 9 percent in the white race in both 1960 and in 1950. At one time or another, 56 percent of Negro children receive aid to dependent children as compared with 2 percent of the white children. Behind these cold statistics lies a mass of unskilled labor and the collapse of the father's role as head of the Negro family in the technological revolution of life. As John D. Pamfret, of *The New York Times News Service,* says in a discerning report, "A middle-class group [of Negroes] has managed to save itself, but for vast numbers of unskilled, poorly educated city working class, the fabric of conventional social relationships has all but collapsed" (*The Courier-Journal,* Louisville, Kentucky, Tuesday, July 20, 1965).

The churches have only begun to be aware of the need for social workers with both theological and social-work training who can cope with this collapse. Protestant counseling as we know it has yet to touch the hem of the garment to heal. For by its very assumptions that people must take initiative, come to an office, and ask for help, pastoral counseling as described to date is a prim, upper-middle-class phenomenon.

3. Enter his frame of reference. We have learned something from pastoral counseling indispensable for our relationship, not only to the Negro, but to people of all races, social classes, and religions other than our own. Carl Rog-

ers has called this "entering the internal frame of reference" of the other person. Martin Buber calls it "experiencing the other side." The Germans call it *Einführung,* or "feeling into" the situation of another. Some of the existentialists call it "seeing the person from within himself the way the person sees himself from within himself." Once we do this with a Negro, a group of Negroes, or a Negro family, we are not the same again. This is the self-emptying of which Paul spoke. A Catholic priest who chose to live among Negroes said it well in a sermon on "The Uncomfortable Christ."

> In that part of Christ's Body called Selma, Alabama, I held the hand of the uncomfortable Christ, that of a minister trembling with fear but bursting with courage. I saw the face of the uncomfortable Christ, that of a boy beaten, scarred externally and internally by the fists of man's hate. . . . I saw the tears of Christ, those of parents panicked by fear for their children. I heard the cries of Christ, those of a people jeered at, bruised, gassed, and in pain. I saw the blood of Christ, that of a little girl. His blood became her blood as it poured from her head onto the side of my face.
>
> I had found the uncomfortable Christ — the Christ of today is as He ever was. And certainly, He exists all around us." (Sermon by Father Maurice Oullet given at St. Michael's College in Winooski, Vermont; quoted in John Cogley, "Religion: Churches and Rights," *The New York Times,* Sunday, August 8, 1965.)

CHAPTER 4

PASTORAL COUNSELING AND THE
CONTEMPORARY SEXUAL REVOLUTION

IN THE SEVENTEENTH century of Nathaniel Hawthorne's
The Scarlet Letter, a Puritan New England community
could ritualistically stamp " A " for adultery on the fore-
head of an unwed mother, isolate her and her child, and
" use " her as a horrible example for others. But even as
early as 1850, when Hawthorne first published *The Scarlet
Letter,* we find the tornness of American culture about the
kind of ethical confusion and ambiguity underneath the
easy " either-or " morality that stamps " A " for adultery
and, I suppose, " S-R " more secretly for self-righteousness
on the rest of the community. For, you will remember, it
was the minister himself who shared in the conception of
the child out of wedlock. Dimmesdale represented Hawthorne's revolutionary ethic which challenged Puritanism
within the gates of the Hebrew-Christian ethic itself.
Though Hawthorne portrays Roger Chillingworth as an
unworthy " leech," he was the physician to whom the
" emaciated, white-cheeked minister with his low, dark and
misshapen figure " went with his burden of guilt. It was
Dimmesdale, who like modern pastoral counselors, said to
the medical doctor: " You deal not, I take it, in medicine
for the soul! " (Nathaniel Hawthorne, *The Scarlet Letter,*
p. 141; Pocketbooks, Inc.). The physician in return said:
" Would you, therefore, that the physician heal the bodily

evil? How may this be, unless you first lay open to him the wound or trouble in your soul? " (*Ibid.*)

But in his Protestant self-sufficiency, Dimmesdale said " with a kind of fierceness " that he would turn to " no earthly physician," but only to God, who could kill or cure as he pleased. He accused the doctor of meddling between the sufferer and his God. In the end, the minister died, making his confession. Hester, the adulteress, became the one to comfort and counsel, especially the women, and to hold out the hope to them of " some brighter period " when, " in Heaven's own time, a new truth would be revealed in order to establish the whole relation between men and women on a surer ground of mutual happiness " (*ibid.*, p. 275).

This " surer ground of mutual happiness " is the concern of this writer. However, the ambiguity and uncertainty of today's sexual ethics require patience, humility, and long-suffering in the pastoral care of persons with sexual problems. This unsureness has usually been avoided by Christians. In order *not* to meet women at the well, in order to be clean of the mongrel race of Samaritans, we as Christians have too often joined that group of Jews who cross over the Jordan and get to Jerusalem ourselves without having anything to do with sexual offenders. Even if we have not avoided the ambiguity and ethical uncertainty in all human codes of sexual morality, we have redoubled our efforts to give simple answers to complex problems. Having lost touch with the Holy Spirit, we fanatically " enforce " the old codes of rural and small-town cultures. These codes simply shove our unsureness under the rug of the manse, the parsonage, or the rectory. All the while, the " secular ethic " of sexual behavior develops in isolation from, and out of communication with, the formal structures of the church and its ministry. The emergence of pastoral counseling, family-life education, and significant literature on the ethics of sex represents a hopeful attempt to bridge the gap between a secular sexual revolution and a static Christian morality.

FACTORS IN THE LOSS OF COMMUNICATION ON SEXUAL PROBLEMS

Segmentation of "Religion" from Life as a Whole

Several factors account at least in part for the " gap " I have just mentioned. First, the nineteenth-century *putsch* of American denominations to accommodate the church to the streets, the ridges, and the crossroads where only a few families lived produced a " larger family " of the local church. The patriarchs of those little churches arbitrated " private matters " such as " sex " outside the church. The preacher — usually nonresident or itinerant — was not consulted.

Second, Gaustad points out that the formation of these churches into competing, ecclesiastical power structures dislocated them for decades from any clear conception of the church as the body of Christ in all its unity. Thus, the churches were only a portion of life itself and " made no effort to direct or control all of the life of the communicant, but only a segment thereof (Edwin S. Gaustad, *Historical Atlas of Religion in America,* p. x; Harper & Row, Publishers, Inc., 1962). This segment made a specialty of religion and a nonreligious, secular concern of sex and the family, for these have nothing to do with " being saved," being converted, or building churches.

However, the pastors of the churches nevertheless visit in homes, interview persons from both within and without their own congregations. They must in some manner cope with the problems of sexual behavior — premarital, marital, and extramarital. Hence, pastoral counseling becomes the rather shaky, swinging bridge over the chasm between these " secular " concerns of the people, on the one hand, and the absorbing task of keeping the church as an institution going and the denomination as a whole comparing fairly well with his fellow minister's competitive enterprise down the street. In their counseling, on pastoral calls, and on the " grapevine," the pastors come into contact with all manner of ethically ambiguous and unsure issues in the personal lives of their confidantes. But in their public, visible ministry, they feel compelled by their people to mouth the platitudes of a simplex, legalistic moralism.

Urban Anonymity

A second factor in the churches' loss of communication on sexual ethics among people is the increase of anonymity and loss of face-to-face relationships among city dwellers. At one and the same time, this lays the plot for many of the sexual variations from small-town and rural norms.

Plato tells the story of a young shepherd who found a magic ring that made him unknown to everyone. Prior to this he was a very righteous and good man. After his discovery that he could be anonymous at will, he lost all semblance of morality. The small-town and rural community denies anonymity to the individual. Everyone knows and tends to watch and care about what everyone else does. This fences the individual within a certain external conformity to public codes of behavior. The face-to-face nature of the community produces a durable kind of relationship between people that tends to make sexual behavior more conventional. However, a favorite theme of contemporary novels such as Lewis' *Cass Timberlane,* Metalious' *Peyton Place,* and Alan Paton's *Too Late the Phalarope* convincingly portrays three things. First, they show the ways in which large cities become places to which rural and small-town people go for a moratorium on their conventional sexual mores. Second, they reflect the ways in which even in the small towns rigid sexual codes are far more a matter of appearance than of reality. In the third place, they reveal how far out of touch with the real guilts and anguishes of people the church and ministry of the " successful " denominations are. The down-and-out sects such as the Holy Rollers, the local physicians and lawyers, and the bartenders are much more the heroes of these novels than are the ministers.

A Growing Secular Ethic of Sex

The people who accept responsibility for the helping process in a given area of human distress tend to provide the raw material for the public's attitude on the ethics involved. This is true of sexual morality. Physicians, particularly psychotherapists, social workers, sociologists, and college teachers have had to accept much of the responsibility for caring for persons with sexual difficulties. The things these scientists have discovered have provided the raw materials for an emerging " secular " sexual ethic. When contrasted with contemporary religious teaching about sexual behavior, this secular ethic does not equivocate about the ambiguity and unsureness in the conventionally stated Christian ethic of sex. It is as clear about the lack of mutual happiness between men and women as was Hester Prynne. I have carefully used the words " conventionally stated Christian ethic of sex." This marks a difference between modern cultural interpretations of sex and the hardheaded realism about sex found in the Old and New Testaments.

Whereas the findings of scientists have provided raw material for an emerging sexual ethic, these same findings are being used by popular magazine writers and publishers of books to create a profitable consumer-reader audience. As such, scientific findings are taken out of the context of the meaning in which the data were discovered. Their original context is lost. In turn, a public that is untrained in the scientific methods whereby the data were found draws its own conclusions as to the meaning of the data. The end result of this, culturally, is a revolution in the sexual mores of our people, both rural and urban. The substance and process of this revolution in sexual attitudes and behavior can now be described in detail.

The Substance and Process of the Sexual Revolution

Novelists, poets, and dramatists of today herald a social revolution. They have the literary drills necessary to pierce beneath the surface of the private and public display of behavior in sex. They are prophetic in the foretelling sense of the word. I have suggested that as early as 1850 the challenge of the Puritan ethic of sex was vivid in Nathaniel Hawthorne's novel *The Scarlet Letter*. More recently, novelists such as James Joyce and Henry Miller have added their bit to presaging the contemporary sexual revolution.

But probably the most persuasive challenger of Christianity at the level of personal morality of all varieties was Friedrich Nietzsche. He averred that ethically the peoples of the world have " a thousand and one goals." No people can " live without valuing," he says. The constant factor in human nature is the *valuing* process itself. The particular codes produced by a people are relative. These differ from neighbor to neighbor. In fact, the *differing* itself is one way a particular group survives. Thus, Nietzsche says: " Much that passed for good with one people was regarded with scorn and contempt by another; thus I found it. Much I found here called bad, which was there decked with purple honors." (Friedrich Nietzsche, *Thus Spake Zarathustra,* p. 57; Tudor Publishing Company, 1934.)

The college student of today does not find this hard to believe. His Christian father advises him to keep himself from sexual intercourse before marriage. Here this is bad. But with a group of fellow college students, even if he agrees with his father, he may never voice his reaction. As one report by Kirkendall says: "When a bunch of fellows get to talking about sex, you're not going to be the one to throw a towel on the fun." Here this is good. (Lester A. Kirkendall, *Premarital Intercourse and Interpersonal Relationships,* p. 34; The Julian Press, Inc., 1961.) With a girl he is hoping to marry, sexual relationships may be bad. With one for whom he has no respect and may never see again, to be successful in his conquest of her is to be "decked with purple honors." Nietzsche speaks scornfully of the "pale criminals" who "have their virtue in order to live long, and in wretched self-complacency." He cherishes only what a person writes with his blood. He finds this blood to be spirit. He disclaims a halfhearted morality which, if made wholehearted, would make heretics out of Christian invalids! (Nietzsche, *op. cit.,* p. 36.)

The dark aphorisms of such a philosophical and poetic atmosphere as this provided a spirit of the age for the scientific papers of Sigmund Freud. Popular opinion — with much financial benefit accruing to American mass media in the process — has made a sort of sex-centered caricature of Freud. Much to the contrary, he was an almost austere and ascetic devotee of his work as a therapist and a ruthless explorer of his own thought processes. Seemingly, his other concerns were the devoted care of his family, a voluminous correspondence with friends, and the study of the psycho-social dimensions of the Jewish religion.

However, his paper entitled "Civilized Sexual Morality and Modern Nervousness," published first in 1908 and published in England in 1942, is a moving force in the contemporary sexual revolution.

Freud says that when civilization's moral demands taboo " every sexual activity other than that in legitimate matrimony . . . the number of strong natures who openly rebel will be immensely increased: and likewise the number of weaker natures will take refuge in neurosis " (Sigmund Freud, *Collected Papers,* Vol. II, p. 87; London: Hogarth Press, 1942). Then he identifies the ways in which " civilized sexual morality by defining the purpose of sexual behavior as procreation and tabooing birth control severely restricts sexuality even within marriage." The complexity is increased by the double standard of morality for men as over against that for women. The end result is a plethora of healthy, immoral men and moral, unhealthy women. Among other alternatives are homosexuality and sexual incompetence of both men and women as husbands and wives within marriage.

In one poignant sentence, Freud summarizes the self-defeating nature of civilized sexual morality: " They strike at the roots of the conditions of preparation for marriage, which according to the intentions of civilized sexual morality should after all be the sole heir of all sexual tendencies " (*ibid.,* p. 96).

In conclusion, Freud raises the question " whether our ' civilized sexual morality ' is worth the sacrifice it imposes upon us." He positively urges a sexual morality that includes " a certain degree of individual happiness among the aims of our cultural development." He recognizes at the same time the need for avoiding pure hedonism as an ethic. Yet he says that " it is certainly not the physician's business to come forward with proposals for reform " (*ibid.*, p. 99).

We cannot understand Freud's total view of sexual morality without calling attention to the fact that he was a Jew. They are a people who do not segment sex from the rest of life. They have ways of teaching about marriage and family living not yet appreciated or devised by Puritan-ancestored Protestants of America. Their Scriptures are, according to Epstein, Mace, and others, much more realistic in their sexual morality than ours. They view sex as one of the " good things " with which God satisfies the desires of mankind. They place upon men far more specific responsibility for their sexual behavior as men than does Protestantism.

As this is being written, the telephone has just interrupted. A pastor on the other side of my city was eager to combine a program of family-life instruction with a revival he is planning for the spring. He says that he " approaches it with fear and trembling because the people do not see much connection between family life and preparation for marriage, on the one hand, and religious confession and commitment on the other." This kind of schism of religion and morality would be foreign to a Jewish rabbi even today. Freud grew up in a Jewish home with respect for the Old Testament, and no evaluation of his positions about sexual morality is clear without including this. For example, few Americans can imagine that Freud actually condemned the premarital petting habits of Americans as a futile, useless, and purposeless pastime of idle people.

A more recent scientific study of sexual behavior, especially that of Americans during and shortly after World War II and the Korean War, is the Kinsey study. The statistical approach was used with a descriptive intention

on the part of the authors. They strictly denied any intention of prescribing norms for sexual behavior. However,
this is exactly what took place. The varieties of sexual
behavior, the practice of premarital and extramarital intercourse, and the extent of these variations from the conventional Christian norm were described in detail. A considerable part of our population took descriptions as norms
for human action. Statistical sophistication is missing among
Americans, but the deification of the statistical occurrence
of what *does* happen as that which *should* happen is common. For example, 39 percent of American males were
found by Kinsey at some time to have participated in
homosexual activity. However, these data were collected
during wartime. Great portions of the population were
segregated from the opposite sex. Moreover, psychiatrists
distinguish homosexual experimentation of the young from
homosexuality that is the overt, preferred behavior of adults.
These major discernments of professional people are missed
entirely by the layman reading the Kinsey reports.

COMMERCIAL PUBLICATION
AND THE SEXUAL REVOLUTION

These scientific efforts called attention to the sexual variety and discontent of thought and action among people.
The field of commercial publication itself has at the same
time been undergoing a revolution. Technological skill in
printing and distributing reading matter inexpensively
makes the Kinsey reports available to people at drugstore
and discount house prices. Novels and psychotherapeutic
commentaries setting forth the points of view of scientists
in watered-down, abbreviated, and overdramatized form
have made the " secular ethic " of the " secular city " more

of a prevailing sexual ethos within and without the church than we are either aware of or willing to admit.

One of the outstanding examples of this is the work of the publisher Hugh Hefner. Forty years old and the son of devout Methodists, he moved between 1953 and 1965 from a rather meager existence to the position of "king" of a $70,000,000 empire of magazines, key clubs, and other *Playboy* enterprises. As *Life* magazine puts it, "It is all built on the female body: the bare 'Playmates' in the magazine and the barely clad 'Bunnies' in the clubs." He was married once, is the father of two children, but is divorced. His present life is now absorbed in his work and in nondurable relationships to first one girl and then another. Diana Lurie, writing of "Hefnerland," says that in this land,

> a woman is simply another aspect of the status-symbol mania which is stamped all over *Playboy*. She is no more or less important than the sleekest sports car or most expensive bottle of Scotch. A woman becomes depersonalized, an object for man's pleasure, something to pour his drinks, inflate his ego and look gorgeous on his arm as he parades in front of his pals (Diana Lurie, "In Hefnerland, Women Are Status Symbols," *Life,* Vol. 59, No. 18 [October 29, 1965], p. 70).

Puritanism seeks to make sex simple and solvable with a legalistic code. In doing so the Puritan who is still with us winds up with scorn and bitterness and avoids the sorrow, the awe, and the reverence that comes from suffering with the complexities and ambiguities of sexual behavior.

Hugh Hefner thinks of the Puritan ethic as "irrational to assume that . . . sexual problems have been dealt with satisfactorily with a few simple rules." In doing so, he becomes a Puritan-in-reverse by coming up with a "few simple rules " of his own. He feels that there is a justifiable place outside of wedlock for sexual intercourse. He justifies this place on several rules of a " game " of sex between man and women. In this he develops a " fun morality " of sex. This is a game that can be " played " so long as no one " gets hurt." He assumes that the old ways in which people " get hurt " — pregnancy and venereal disease — are outmoded. Religious interpretation, according to Hefner, is out of his province. Hefner says that " it would be a mistake to think " of his philosophy of sex as a " conflict between secular and religious interest in society." Yet in another installment of his " philosophy " he invokes the doctrine of the separation of church and state in his behalf. He complains that Puritanism has " so infiltrated our secular society . . . that we have failed to maintain the free democracy " that the founding fathers such as " Washington, Jefferson, Madison, Franklin and the rest of those first American patriots envisioned." This " flip side " attempt at not just separating but hermetically sealing religion from ethical encounter with society *is* secularism.

Paul Carroll, associate editor of *Perspective,* is, in my opinion, right in his evaluation of Henry Miller and, by association, Hugh Hefner. He says they are really Puritans at heart. Instead of flagellating their " corrupt bones as a good Puritan would have done," their heroes exhaust themselves in ceaseless and meaningless sexual orgies. These " bouts are transitory because otherwise there might be a communion " between the contestants or " the woman might become a person, the worst violation of Puritan etiquette." Disgust with the female is at the core of Puritan anger, says Carroll. So Miller and the *Playboy* philosophy of sex deprive women of personality. The end result is a conception of women as various parts of a man's body. Men's encounters with the bizarre women are nightmares of meaningless copulation " with all tenderness frozen out " (Paul Carroll, " Is Miller Really a Puritan? " *Saturday Review,* February 23, 1963, p. 29).

In the Puritan era a woman was seen not as a person but as a potential witch. She was " used " sexually and as a projection screen for the guilty consciences of men. In the *Playboy* era, woman is seen as a " toy " for the games of men, as a " bunny " rabbit to be seen but not met and understood as a person in her own right. In their efforts to correct one form of Puritanism, Hefner and Miller develop a macabre form of their own. They and the Puritans share in common the treatment of women as things to be used rather than persons in their own right.

Similarly, men in both the Puritanism of conventional Protestantism and the reverse-effect Puritanism of Miller and Hefner are seen as *means* and not as persons in their own right. Men in reality are not just means to procreation, social status for women, and financial security in modern suburbia. They are not animals of prey or dispensable items in the home except for the money they bring in to support the growing matriarchal culture of America. They are not just a commercial audience to be stimulated by *Playboy* advertisements, asked to pay the bill, and then told to go home and be good boys. Men, too, are persons in their own right.

The impact of social change and technological advance has resulted, as has been repeatedly underscored, in moral confusion and unsureness. A revolution has occurred that points up the need for a reappraisal of time-honored values. The pastoral counselor walks the shaky, swinging bridge between the time-honored values of absolute chastity before marriage and absolute fidelity after marriage, on the one hand, and the acceptance of the gross national product of sexual behavior of Americans as the norm characteristic of the secular ethic, on the other. Is there a better and more certain ethical construction that will answer Hester Prynne's prayer for a " surer ground of mutual happiness " between men and women?

A Pastoral Counselor's Ethical Reconstruction Amid the Sexual Revolution

As a pastoral counselor, I have faced the ethical ambiguities described by authors since 1850. I have talked with single girls who are in love with divorced men. They will not marry them because their Puritan parents and brothers reject the idea of their marrying divorced men. Yet they have sexual relations with the divorced men outside of marriage. I have talked with middle-aged men who continue to expect sexual enjoyment from their wives, but whose wives feel that now that their children are grown sex relations are wrong. I have seen these marriages blow up in divorce.

Harvey Cox bluntly poses the dilemma with which pastoral counselors are faced when he says in his book, *The Secular City,* " Premarital sexual conduct should therefore serve to strengthen the chances of sexual success and fidelity in marriage, and we must face the real question of whether avoidance of intercourse beforehand is always the best preparation " (Harvey Cox, *The Secular City,* p. 215; The Macmillan Company, 1964). The principle of complete chastity and avoidance of premarital intercourse is a Christian ideal that I cherish and teach both publicly and privately. However, the principle can be distorted by a schism between " sacred " and " sexy " women in the perception of men. The principle can be validated on both " secular " and " sacred " grounds. The principle is not the private possession of Christians. The bad preparation for marriage in the " enforcement " of the principle of premarital chastity arises out of the distortions of a double standard of morality — one for men and another for women — and the failure of adults to establish clear communication with their children about sex as a normal part of life.

For example, one does not have to be a Christian to take issue with Harvey Cox when he assumes that medical advances in antibiotics and contraceptives " will soon remove the last built-in deterrents to premarital coitus." The American Medical Association reports that 1.1 million Americans are venereally infected annually — about 3,000 a day. In some urban areas the number of cases has increased from 200 to 800 percent in the last four-year period. The cases of infectious syphilis have almost tripled in the last five years (news release, *Louisville Times,* September 3, 1965). The family publication of the American Medical Association, *Today's Health,* points out that 56 percent of a 1,300 sample of these persons were between the ages of fifteen and twenty. The magazine points out that many of these were from privileged and respectable families: " *Nice* people and *nice* kids from *nice* families contract venereal disease — syphilis and gonorrhea — by the thousands " (G. Edward Maxwell, " Why the Rise in Teen-age Venereal Disease? " *Today's Health,* Vol. 43, No. 4 [September, 1965], p. 19).

The efficacy of modern contraception of which Cox speaks is also only partial. Clark Vincent's definitive studies; of unmarried mothers points out that between 1938 and 1958 the number of births per 1,000 unmarried women of childbearing age rose from 7 to 21. " Contrary to popular opinion the rate increased least among the women aged between fifteen to nineteen (108 percent) and most among women aged between twenty-five and twenty-nine (453 percent)." However, the number — not the rate — of " unwed mothers aged between fifteen and nineteen during the 1960's is more than twice that in the 1950's simply because there are more people in the age group" (Clark Vincent, *Unmarried Mothers,* pp. 1–8; The Free Press of Glencoe, Inc., 1961).

Among the many contributing factors in this is the age-old effort of the girls to bind their sexual partners into a more lasting relationship and the prevailing "philosophy of fun morality" in child-rearing practices. In other words, it is all right to have "fun" but not all right to "get too serious." Sex thus becomes a game. It *may* be — as Eric Berne has said — one of those games in which no one gets hurt or in which no one is irremediably hurt. Or again it *may* be one of those games "which ends in the surgery, the courtroom or the morgue." In other words, as Seward Hiltner has said, sex is serious, and, to quote Berne, a game that is played "for keeps" (Eric Berne, *The Games People Play: The Psychology of Human Relationships,* p. 64; Grove Press, Inc., 1964).

The lethal quality of this "fun morality" or mistaken gamesmanship approach to sexuality is especially clear in the research of Ehrmann in his study of premarital dating behavior. (Winston W. Ehrmann, *Premarital Dating Behavior,* p. 269; Holt, Rinehart & Winston, Inc., 1959.) The men are playing a game different from that which the women are playing, with different rules and different goals — in other words, a different morality. The girl engages in premarital sexual intercourse *with the hope of a durable lasting relationship.* The boy does so with the *fear* of a durable relationship. The girl has been morally schooled to have sexual relationship *only* with someone she loves. The boy has been schooled *not* to do this with someone he loves. This is a diabolical stalemate of relationship that lays the groundwork for distrust and paranoid interaction in marriage if the couple should get married.

All of this tends to be more characteristic of middle-class persons than of either lower- or upper-class persons. But these are, for the most part, the people who go to church. Pastoral counseling itself has been too largely restricted to work with the middle classes. Most of our studies of sex are of middle-class college students, not the general population. When we start summarizing a workable Christian ethic for the pastoral care of persons with sexual problems, we must be deep enough and clear enough to be heard and understood by all classes — the literate and the illiterate, the upwardly mobile and the downtrodden alike.

In summary, then, what is a positive pastoral ethic for the working pastor to practice and to teach among those who seek his aid as a counselor?

A Pastoral Counselor's Reconstruction of a Positive Christian Sexual Ethic

The secular revolution has shattered the Puritan sexual ethic. In the process it has produced a secular ethic that is just as guilty of removing the ambiguity and uncertainty inherent in responsible sexual behavior as were and are the Puritans. Hester Prynne's prayer for a "surer ground of mutual happiness" between men and women in both instances requires reconstruction. One ethic is as shattering to human life as is the other. Both sacrifice a part of humanity in behalf of another. They both lack mutuality and do not produce happiness in its deepest sense. Several dimensions of that "surer ground" for mutual relations between men and women stand out in a positive reconstruction.

First, both Biblically and clinically the ambiguity and

uneasiness related to sexual behavior are inherent in *any* exercise of power, of which sexual power is just one example. This cannot be "edited out" by a scribal emendation of human nature. Simple rules such as absolute chastity, or virginity, before marriage and absolute fidelity after marriage focus Christian ethics off-center of man's continual need of forgiveness and growth in Christ.

Therefore, the pastoral counselor begins with an awareness of his own humanity, a knowledge of his temptation to use simple rules as a means to exercise power and "lord it over" the flock. He recognizes and accepts himself as a sexual being who could no more stand the awesome judgment of God than could his counselee. Whereas purity of life and fidelity to one's partner are important principles, they are no substitute for God or for forgiveness. "Principles," as Harvey Cox says, "are useful and perhaps indispensable in ethical thinking, but all too often 'sticking to principles' can become just another way to avoid seeing persons. It can signify a relapse from Gospel into Law." (Cox, *op. cit.*, p. 215.)

In the second place, if we are going to stick to principles — and I think we need to do so without playing God — we need a value framework that combines all that we know about life — not just that which has been classified as "secular" or "sacred." I am in hearty agreement with Friedrich Sieburg's position, as quoted by Helmut Thielicke, on this point:

> It is the task of pastoral care in this area to communicate this interpretation. That is to say, pastoral care must point out what one makes of his erotic partner when he isolates bios and person from each other (namely, a selfishly misused function-bearer); and inversely, it must show that he separates person and bios from each other when he allows certain forms of sex to have power over him. But pastoral care will move on *this* level of thought

and interpretation in the positive sense too; it will not attempt to combat the insistent libido with the moral appeal: "You dare not do this"; because this appeal does not touch the root of the problem at all and is therefore fruitless. The Law reaches only the "outside of the cup and of the plate" (Matt. 23:25 ff.) and not always even this; but it certainly never reaches the "inside." The libido can be attacked only by the kind of pastoral care which is aware of the anthropological problem and challenges the person to engage in a particular kind of meditation or exercise of his own thinking. The aim of this meditation is to arrive at the conviction that the desired body belongs to the "being" of a human being who himself belongs to another; a human being, that is, who has been bought with a price (I Cor. 6:20; 7:23), and has a temporal and eternal destiny, a destiny in which one who claims this other person in his totality responsibly participates. Only through this meditation do we come to see that *whole* human being, who alone is capable of disclosing the full richness of sexuality. For among the conclusions of our study will be the realization that focusing one's intention upon the whole man, upon his indivisible unity, does not merely curb sex, but rather liberates it and brings it to its fullness. (Cf. Friedrich Sieburg, "Vom Unfug der Entblössung," in *Constance* [1951], p. 9; quoted in Helmut Thielicke, *The Ethics of Sex,* pp. 24–25; Harper & Row, Publishers, Inc., 1964.)

Such a value framework would, on the basis of a number of empirical studies, embrace several principles of sexual behavior.

1. *The principle of "knownness" between men and women.* The book of Proverbs speaks of "strange women" who are "loose." The studies of Kirkendall demonstrate how responsibility and trust in even premarital sexual relations increased dramatically when the couple knew each other, and were not strangers and anonymous to each other. Quaintly enough, "to know" is a verb translated out of the Hebrew in many Biblical statements to refer to

sexual behavior. Kirkendall's study of 200 college students analyzed the six different levels or qualities of premarital relationships. Levels I and II were those with prostitutes and pickups in which identities were either nonexistent, extremely casual, or temporary. Communication, if it existed at all, was mostly nonverbal. However, at levels III, IV, V, and VI the persons were known to each other as casual acquaintances, in dating, courtship, and engagement situations. Communication was enhanced as the level of "knownness" increased. The pastor who establishes a private, confessional relationship of trust with persons who actually participate in premarital intercourse must have an eye to see and a heart to sense the differences in these intermediate shades of gray between right and wrong. Pastoral patience is required of the minister if he is to *inspire* a person toward the ideals that he himself cherishes. The ideal of purity can be inspired, but to "lay it down as a law" invites rebellion.

2. *The principle of integrity in relationships as opposed to deceit and duplicity*. Sexual struggle on the part of women and men is often a symptom of their difficulty in establishing relationships of openness and truthfulness with each other. Marital infidelity is often called "cheating." Unexpressed distrust of a partner is the beginning of a paranoid interaction that closes communication. The partners soon seek "understanding" elsewhere, inasmuch as they cannot trust each other. Trust — basic trust — is the foundation of any covenant. The detached person does not form covenants. To do so requires that one become known. To become known is to obligate oneself.

3. *The principle of care for the partner as a person as opposed to the "use" of the partner as a means*. A woman with definite intent to "use" a man to become pregnant — whether married or unmarried — and with no "use" for

him as a person "uses" him and does not care for him. The man who uses a woman for his own satisfaction within or without marriage with no care for her as a person in her own right violates this principle. The Kantian definition of personality is to the point here. Kant says that everything in creation except personality "can be used by man as a means to an end; but man himself . . . is an end in himself" (Immanuel Kant, "Kritik der praktischen Vernunft," *Gesammelte Schriften,* Book V, p. 87; Reimer-Verlag, 1908). Any other kind of relationship tends to be exploitative and destructive of integrity.

4. *The principle of responsibility*. Sexual behavior is measured ethically not so much by "how far who goes with whom" as how much responsibility each is willing to take for his own behavior. The social caseworker with unmarried mothers to counsel sees fathers of pregnant girls as more intent on hurting the boy who "ruined" their daughter than they are to accept responsibility for their destitute daughter's medical care. A husband may actually "nudge" his wife into sexual adventures with other men because of his own sexual inability or irresponsibility. A woman may want all the "rights and privileges" of marriage but steadfastly refuse to accept sexual responsibility toward her husband. As one young girl said to her yet uncommitted boyfriend who demanded sexual intercourse of her:

I am a woman, not a toy. You can go as far with me as you are willing to take responsibility for having gone, because I love you and don't want to lose you. But I am willing to lose you if you are not man enough to treat me as a woman and not a plaything, to accept as much responsibility for me as I am willing to accept for you. When you decide about these things, you can see me again and not until then.

5. *The principle of durability.* Harry Stack Sullivan says that one of the marks of a mature person is the capacity to form and maintain durable relationships. This is the hidden agenda going on in all sexual relationships beyond the crassest ones of prostitution and the most casual kinds of " pickups." Even in these relationships, hidden elements of durability have been seen to grow into lasting relationships of forgiveness, integrity, and responsibility. I have seen this happen clinically and have always wished that I had a good explanation of the events of Rahab's life!

Durability is expressed Biblically in two ways: One is the overcoming of all that would separate us. Nothing " will be able to separate us from the love of God in Christ Jesus our Lord." Erich Fromm, in his book *The Art of Loving,* puts it well when he says: " *The awareness of human separation, without reunion by love, is the source of shame. It is at the same time the source of guilt and anxiety* " (Erich Fromm, *The Art of Loving,* p. 9; Harper & Brothers, 1956).

The second way durability is expressed Biblically is in the resurrection. Here, as Browning says, death itself is dead. The ambiguities and uncertainties of life are clarified both now and later. Jesus says that in the resurrection there is neither marriage nor giving in marriage. Here we " know fully even as we are already known." The foundation of a distinctly Christian ethic of sex can never be less than the death, burial, and resurrection of Christ. Any static statement of law misses Jesus' intention. The resurrection transcends the durability of marriage with a high durability of God's own making.

Anton T. Boisen died on October 1, 1965, at the age of 89. He was the founder of the modern pastoral-care movement in America. He lived his life as a bachelor, though his autobiography reveals that he loved one woman all his life. He endured three psychotic breakdowns. In his autobiography, he tells the following story of his love for and separation from this woman as it depicts his sense of God's intention and yet his acceptance of his suffering. He says of her:

> My love for Alice Batchelder has been for me a source of healing. . . . I am thinking of the old Dante-Beatrice story, in which the poet had to pass through the fire before he could enter Paradise and join the woman he worshiped. I am thinking of Professor Hocking's insistence that love between man and woman can be truly happy only when each is a free and autonomous being, dependent not upon the other but upon God. Where, on the other hand, a man's love for a woman is such that he draws not from the common source of strength, but clings to her, that man is not worthy of her. That principle is sound, and it may help in the interpretation of the experience of 1920. It was necessary for me to pass through the purgatorial fires of a horrifying psychosis before I could set foot in my promised land of creative activity. (Anton T. Boisen, *Out of the Depths: An Autobiographical Study of Mental Disorder and Religious Experience,* pp. 207–208; Harper & Brothers, 1960.)

The resurrection does not ignore the psychological criterion of durability as that " sure ground of mutual happiness " between man and woman. But it catches it up and raises it to a transcendent power. Thus, the secular and the religious, like male and female, become one in Christ.

As this chapter closes, the reader may ask: " In discussing principles for sexual behavior, I kept expecting you to mention the Seventh Commandment: 'Thou shalt not commit adultery.' But you did not, and I wondered why? "

In the first place, let me say that I did discuss it positively but not negatively. I said: " Purity of life and fidelity to one's partner are important principles, but they are no substitute for God or for forgiveness." All the negative commandments are subordinate to the one commandment to love God above all else. In a certain sense, one may worship one's wife or husband or lover to the exclusion of God. He or she may be absolutely faithful sexually to the spouse. But even such worship itself can be said to be adultery. Or, to make sex the be-all and end-all of life, married or single, is adultery, a form of idolatry. We cannot serve two masters.

But even more specifically than this, when we use the Seventh Commandment as the *apex* of our Christian morality of sex, we ignore the act of God in Jesus Christ to forgive even the adulterer. We convey a negative ethic that drives the offender from us rather than establishes his confidence in us. Then sin works through the law to make him all the more sinful.

Therefore, I have chosen to state the positive principles of *any* faithful Christian relationship. The sexual relationship is the most demanding example. These principles are: the principle of knownness versus anonymity; the principle of integrity and openness versus deceit; the principle of caring for a partner versus using him; the principle of responsibility versus irresponsibility; the principle of durability versus separation and estrangement. Then I chose to relate this ethic to the Christian belief in the resurrection rather than to tie it to the Decalogue.

To break these principles or to ignore them in any relationship is adultery. Such breakage leads to adulteration, duplicity, and divorce. Any relationship, be it sexual or not, especially that of man to God, can become adulterous in this way. When we break these principles — Christian or secular — we contribute to a wicked and adulterous generation.

CHAPTER 5

PASTORAL COUNSELING AND THE
REMARRIAGE OF DIVORCEES

S AFE PLACES to hide disappear when the Biblical, historical, systematic, and pastoral theologian alike is asked: " What is the responsibility of a pastor to the divorcee who requests remarriage of him and his church? " This question confronts the church and its ministry, as G. H. Hoffman, a Lutheran pastor in California, has said, with " the task of defining our ultimate aim in dealing with people." What is the purpose of the church and its ministry? This question becomes specific. No room remains for glittering generalities when we ask the church and its pastors to care for the divorced person who seeks remarriage and acceptance into the Christian community as a fellowship. Social dilemma is the atmosphere of such pastoral care.

In order to see the pastoral care of divorcees clearly and perform this ministry wisely, three things must be done here. First, we must assess the nature and extent of remarriage of divorced persons as a pattern within contemporary American family life. Second, we must evaluate the various ways that the problem of remarriage of divorcees is being met by churches today. And, third, we must arrive at a point of view that can be a basis for conversation with other interested and concerned persons and serve as a guide for concrete Christian action in the pastoral care of the divorcee who is or is being remarried.

REMARRIAGE OF DIVORCEES: AN EMERGING WAY OF LIFE

Remarriage is the pattern of action taken by the pro-
nounced majority of divorcees. In William J. Goode's study
of 425 divorced women, he found that 94 percent of the
women aged thirty and below remarry. Also, he found
that 54 percent of his sample had remarried within 26
months after their divorce and 50 percent of the rest had
a steady date. (William J. Goode, *After Divorce,* p. 207;
The Free Press of Glencoe, Inc., 1956.) Jessie Bernard, in
her intensive study of remarriage of all kinds, points out
that six sevenths of those divorcing at any one time remarry within fourteen years. In "Utopolis," a study which
she reports, 14 percent remained unmarried after divorce,
33 percent were "recidivists," or repeaters, who were divorced and remarried again and again, demonstrating "divorce proneness" and the lack of aptitude in marital life. (Jessie S. Bernard, *Remarriage: A Study of Marriage,* pp. 107–
108; The Dryden Press, Inc., 1956.) Fifty-three percent of
the couples in the study of those remarried seemed from
all indices available to be as happy as, or happier than,
couples who had never been divorced.

Thomas P. Monohan's study of the stability of remar-
riages demonstrated that the divorce ratio increases with
each marriage in a sequence of divorces. "Second marriages
ending in divorce show a shorter duration than first marriages. With each prior experience with divorce, the duration of the remarriage ending in divorce becomes shorter."
(Thomas P. Monohan, "The Duration of Marriage in
Relation to Divorce," *Marriage and Family Living,* Vol 1,
No. 2 [May, 1959], p. 138.) Wisconsin statistics from 1867–
1957, according to Monohan, reveal that the mean duration
of marriages from the time of the wedding to the time of
divorce was ten years. From the time of marriage to separa-

tion was eight years. Therefore, in overemphasizing divorce, we may overlook the fact that the average person, at least in Wisconsin, was separated from his or her spouse for two full years before the time of divorce decrees! Monohan further points out that the common assumption that most divorces occur in the third and fourth years of marriage is misleading when the data concerning separation are examined. The real crisis in these marriages comes in the first and, at most, the second year of marriage. (Thomas P. Monohan, "When Couples Part: Statistical Trends and Relationships in Divorce," *American Sociological Review,* Vol. 27 [October, 1962], pp. 625–633.) All these data can be further illuminated by Goode's findings that 19 percent of the divorcees in his sample were never engaged, 17 percent were engaged less than two months, and 35 percent were engaged for six months or less. This means that 71 percent of them had only a very brief engagement, if any at all, which was further complicated by the fact that 71 percent of the total sample had no premarital guidance at all.

When we put these research studies together, we can conclude several things about the responsibility of the church to the divorced person. *First,* if it is true that over 90 percent of the persons seeking to be married prefer that a minister perform the ceremony, then the church itself has been negligent in giving premarital guidance and counseling aimed at preventing divorce. In this sense, the guilt in divorce is a corporate guilt to be shared by the churches and not to be loaded totally upon the individual couple's backs. *Second,* the church can discharge some of this responsibility by teaching, urging, and requiring a waiting period for those whom it and its pastors join in wedlock. This encouragement of an engagement period would provide time for the couple to test and deepen a relationship into effective permanence for marriage. It would give the church and the pastor an opportunity for instruction, guidance, encouragement, and comfort to the couple in their pilgrimage toward the kind of maturity that marriage requires.

Third, after the couple are married, exceptional attention should be given them during the first two years of marriage. They are most open at this time to instruction, fellowship, and guidance. Realism requires that we admit that much that passes for " premarital counseling " simply does not " take." The couple that seeks premarital counseling is the exception rather than the rule. Therefore, the church can provide these same kinds of guidance after the fact of marriage. This should be done in the critical first two years when most divorces are being set into motion. *Fourth,* even when separation occurs, the church still has a measure of time for preventive ministry. The apostle Paul recognized some of the religious functions of marital separation in I Cor. 7:5 when he suggested that couples come apart for prayer and fasting. Does the church of today have any distinctly religious meanings to apply to a marital separation? Is there, anywhere, an understanding community in which such a separation can take place creatively rather than destructively? Pastoral counseling today can and often does offer this. Some feeble efforts toward retreat centers for distressed married couples are being made. But in the absence of *religious* concern for the well-being of stress-ridden marriages, we can hypothesize that much of the harshness of the churches in the care of divorcees is a tacit confession of the guilt of the church for its timidity, its negligence, and its lack of discipline in attending to the spiritual needs of the couple before marriage, shortly after marriage, and during the period of separation. The suggestions made here, however, presuppose a *disciplined* church. The *divorced Christian* is a symptom of the irresponsibility of the church as a *teaching* community and its failure of nerve as a fellowship of human suffering.

An example of this is cited by Ralph Bridgman, Chief Marriage Counselor of the Family Court Center of Toledo, Ohio. He says:

> In one Ohio jurisdiction served by 375 churches, of the 1,050 applicants for divorce with children under fourteen, during one recent year, nine out of ten listed a church affiliation. Taking a sampling of 45 by telephone inquiry, a court counselor discovered that only two thirds of these names were reported by church secretaries or pastors to be on their church membership or attendance rolls. Of these thirty, only sixteen were known by the church to be in divorce litigation. Regarding the other fourteen, their pastors said: " I never got to know them "; " No, they have never spoken to me of their trouble "; or, " I didn't realize that things had gotten that bad." Regarding the sixteen known to be divorcing, their pastors said: " I've done all I can, and I hope you as a specialist can get somewhere with them "; " They've never talked to me about it "; or, " We just can't reach them." *Only three of these sixteen had been in active counseling with their pastors.*

In this rather lengthy quotation, one can discern the major responsibilities of the church to the separated person prior to divorce action:

1. The church must develop durable relationships to people who " use " the name of the church but have nothing to do with it. One third of this group did just that. At the time of marriage itself, this group may well have turned to the minister to be married " on the spur of the moment " with no previous notice. They tacitly assumed that they had no responsibility to the church beyond possibly paying the minister a fee. They *used* the church at

the time of marriage and later used it as a reference. At
no time had they related themselves dynamically to the
church nor had the church challenged them to do this or
enabled them to feel the persistence of its outreach toward them.

2. The church must learn to communicate with and " get
to know " people in terms of their family crises, especially
crises of conflict and estrangement. The process of marriage
conflict goes through several phases: (a) typical adjust-
mental conflicts over role, communication, continuing
sloughing off of immaturities from childhood, and the use
of time, money, and energy; (b) the serious breach of the
covenant of trust; (c) the stage of private misunderstanding; (d) the stage of social involvement; (e) the stage of
separation; (f) the legal phase; (g) the phase of divorce;
(h) the phase of postdivorce readjustment. Both the pastor
and the church need to be aware of this process, to be
disciplined to detect the subverbal cues of trouble, and to
establish communication and trust between the troubled
person and his church and its minister.

3. The church must train both ministry and laity to deal
competently and responsibly with the problems of families
in trouble. The pastors in several instances in Bridgman's
study were unaware that there was any trouble. In others,
they simply did not feel competent to deal with the problems and hoped that a specialist could " get somewhere
with them " (Ralph P. Bridgman, " Marital Discord, Divorce, and Reconciliation," Pastoral Psychology, Vol. 9,
No. 86 [September, 1959], p. 19).

The serious observer knows that these three ministries
are not taking place, except feebly, within Protestantism.
The church and its ministry, therefore, must share in the
guilt and hardness of heart associated with divorce. We
should not reduce the weight of the sin, condemnation,

and guilt attached to divorce. Rather, we should distribute it and accept our fair share of it. Let him that is without sin cast the first stone at the adulterer!

Additional data are necessary from a cultural and anthropological point of view, however, before our perspective of the task of the church in relation to divorcees is set within the right framework. Margaret Mead and others have called attention to the way in which our culture has more and more defined marriage as a tentative commitment. Americans in considerable numbers enter marriage with a mood of tentativeness. As Mead says, in America, " marriage *may* be for life, *can* be for life, but also may not be." Divorce, she says, " may come to any marriage, no matter how devoted, how conscientious, how much in love each spouse originally was," and " a marriage is something that has to be worked at each day. . . . Both husband and wife face the need to re-choose each other, to reassert and re-establish the never permanent claim of one upon the other's choice." (Margaret Mead, *Male and Female,* pp. 357–358; William Morrow and Company, Inc., 1948.) But, with a mood of tentative commitment, even the normal strains of marriage become unexpected, unpleasant, and unusually strong. Then the couple's first thought is to dissolve the marriage.

In addition to this is our culture's emphasis upon *planned obsolescence.* The mood of our culture is to discard something that will not work and get a new one. Our economy is geared to this newness. When this mood slips over from things to persons, marriage may be looked upon similarly. If the partner is not adjustable, cannot be " fixed," and if the marriage, therefore, does not " work," then the prevailing mood is to trade the unfitting mate for one that does! It is this mood, rather than the idea of " sequential polygamy," or the having of many mates in sequence rather than at the same time, which motivates the American marriage partner to dissolve the marriage. The individual partner holds to the illusion that a day will come when a *perfect* marriage partner will be found, one that does not require continuing growth of him or her. This "eschatological" hope hastens the end of the present, imperfect marriage.

The observation of A. C. Kinsey in his first volume, however, speaks clearly to this mood of our culture: "A preliminary examination of six thousand marital histories in the present study and of nearly three thousand divorce histories suggests that there may be nothing more important in a marriage than a determination that it shall persist." (A. C. Kinsey, W. B. Pomeroy, and C. E. Martin, *Sexual Behavior in the Human Male,* p. 544; W. B. Saunders Company, 1948.) Contrasted with the mood of tentativeness of our culture, the inculcation of this "determination that the marriage shall persist" becomes the major responsibility of the church in both preventing divorces from arising and in dealing with the divorcee who comes for remarriage.

The task of the church in the face of this mood of tentativeness and planned obsolescence is to hold steadfastly to the ideal of marriage set forth by the Lord Jesus Christ: Marriage is a covenant of love and trust between two people. It is a covenant that *should* not be broken, but is broken. It must be renewed daily in prayer and commitment. Love *grows* in all manner of knowledge and insight. The permanence of marriage cannot be confused with stagnation and failure to grow in maturity of commitment. The double responsibility of the church, then, is: (1) to make the ideal of the permanence of marriage both meaningful and attractive to people, on the one hand,

and (2) to repair the damage to this ideal that is done in the processes of ignorance, immaturity, hardness of heart, and abandon to "unmaturity" that eventuates in divorce, on the other hand. But the question now awaits us: How have the churches characteristically gone about discharging this double responsibility?

Pastoral Approaches to the Care of Divorcees in Remarriage

The churches and their pastors have taken four major approaches to the remarriage of divorcees: (1) the laissez-faire approach, (2) the idealistic approach, (3) the forensic approach, and (4) the educational and rehabilitative approach.

The Laissez-faire Approach

The laissez-faire approach to the church's ministry to divorcees takes many forms. Most obvious is the " marrying parson " who marries any and all persons for a fee. He is often the pastor of a church which callously assumes that he will make a part of his living this way. One step removed from this is the pastor who says: " If I don't marry these persons, someone else will." He may even use the thin evangelistic rationalization that this "opens the door for us to win them to Christ." Or he may have a magical conception of the blessing of the church as something that is efficacious in warding off evil from the marriage. He may justify this by sentimentally saying that he does not have the heart to turn away people who want the ministry of the church. Such pastors operate individualistically and make these decisions in isolation from their lay leadership. They usually have had no instruction in the disciplines of pastoral care. They have spent equally little time in learning the Biblical, historical, and ethical perspectives of the problem of divorce growing out of the experience of the church in the past. These persons extend their practice of marrying people to divorced and nondivorced alike. They are oblivious to the superstition in the attitudes of the persons who "want a minister to marry them." They are naïve about the way the church is "used." They do not perceive the detached unrelatedness of some divorcees. They do not diagnose the ways in which detachment is a timed device that will tend to "go off" later and produce another divorce when this marital partner, like the church, is no longer "useful."

The laissez-faire approach to the problems of divorcees appears again in the legalist. He flatly says that he has nothing to do with any divorced person and will not marry them. He justifies his course of action on tightly interpreted Biblical grounds. Nevertheless, he does not extend any kind of ministry to the divorcees apart from telling them that he does not marry divorced persons. This minister often conceives of his task as a very formal one, restricted to the preaching of sermons, the ministration of formal services such as funerals, weddings, etc., and the promotion of the church, with himself as an executive director. He leaves the problems of divorced persons alone, in much the same way that he leaves untouched other complicated social dilemmas which consume pastoral time and attention. Usually the divorced person would not go to him for the very reason that the minister is preoccupied with other matters, and also because of the impersonal nature of his relationship and the kind of preaching that he presents from the pulpit. His preaching is not pastorally oriented. It is a role-protected, institutionally oriented preaching.

The Idealistic Approach

The idealistic approach to the church and its ministry to divorcees is the second approach to divorcees seeking remarriage. These churches and pastors say that the Christian ideal for marriage allows *no* place for remarriage of divorcees by the church and its ministry. Not even the " saving clause " of adultery is accepted as justification for remarriage. The position is that the church cannot allow *any* excuse for divorcees' remarrying. This position was stated most clearly by the Acts of Convocation of the Anglican Church at the Convocation of Canterbury in its regulations concerning marriage and divorce. This statement was adopted in May, 1957:

> (1) . . . according to God's will, declared by our Lord, marriage is in true principle a personal union, for better or for worse, of one man with one woman, exclusive of all others on either side, and indissoluble save by death. (2) . . . as a consequence . . . remarriage after divorce during the lifetime of a former partner always involves a departure from the true principle of marriage as declared by our Lord. (3) . . . in order to maintain the principle of lifelong obligation which is inherent in every legally contracted marriage and is expressed in the plainest terms in the Marriage Service the Church should not allow the use of that Service in the case of anyone who has a former partner still living. (Quoted in A. P. Shepherd, *Marriage Was Made for Man,* p. 13; Methuen & Co., Ltd., 1958, p. 13.)

Many pastors and churches of the free-church tradition as well hold steadfastly to this ideal. They accurately contend, as does Prof. Nolan Howington, that the Biblical record of the teachings of Jesus allows *no* room for remarriage without departing from the ideal of Jesus for Christian marriage. G. F. Fisher, Archbishop of Canterbury, challenges the use of the word " ideal " for this position. He says that our Lord spoke of this " not as an ideal but as what marriage in fact by its nature *is*." Any departure from this inherent nature of marriage is not a failure to attain an ideal, but a departure from real marriage as God ordained it. With this statement of the ideal of the Christian faith for marriage, no church or its pastors can safely disagree. But, as Professor Howington has also said, this ideal is set over against the serious dilemmas of both the divorcee and the church in an imperfect, unideal world. (G. F. Fisher, *Problems of Marriage and Divorce*, p. 8; S.P.C.K., 1955.) Nevertheless, a pastor and church may be committed to bearing witness to the ideal nature of real marriage in the presence of the hardness of heart of an adulterous generation. Still, they take seriously the pastoral care and rehabilitation of the remarried person, even though they do not perform public weddings of such persons. For example, the Convocation of Canterbury set forth a procedure for this. The couple would be married according to civil law. The parish priest would gather all the pertinent information about the couple and present it to the bishop. The bishop in turn would evaluate the information and decide whether the church's witness to our Lord's standard of marriage is preserved and whether the couple is living in good faith with the church and is to be permitted to partake of the Sacraments. His approval is necessary for this. The advantage of this is that it takes and distributes the responsibility and does not leave the parish minister to carry the whole burden. Furthermore, no prohibitions were laid down as to " what private prayers the curate in the exercise of his pastoral ministry may say with the persons concerned." Nor were regulations issued as to " where or when these prayers shall be said " (*ibid.*, p. 15.)

On the other hand, therefore, the idealistic position would

avoid legalism. As Fisher says, whereas Christ was describing marriage as it really is, he did not at the same time legislate concerning divorce in the sense of laying down rules for his church. Therefore, the church must exercise Christian compassion toward the couple, maintain relationship with a love that endures all things, and bring the ministry of rehabilitative prayer and guidance to the couple. Therefore, some Anglicans, such as Bryan Green, have advocated a " service of blessing " for a couple who is remarried by civil authorities. He says that this should be a semiprivate service with only the closest of friends and relatives present. It is made plain that this is not a marriage service. The purpose of such a service is to make it clear that " the Christian Church is firm in its discipline and unshaken in its upholding of the ideal of permanent marriages, and yet at the same time wholeheartedly welcomes to God's forgiveness and to His blessing those who are repentant and determined to live a new life " (J. H. Cruse and B. S. W. Green, *Marriage, Divorce, and Repentance in the Church of England*).

The reason behind the idealistic assumption that there are *no* grounds for justifying remarriage is both psychological and theological. To imply that there is such a thing as an " innocent party " overlooks the psychological intertwining of action and reaction that motivates one or the other party to " commit adultery." Adultery itself may be a symptom of deeper and more murderous impulses. Self-righteousness on the part of the man whose wife has been unfaithful to him can be as fiendish as adultery itself. A pastor is naïve and underestimates the devil himself when he says that adultery is the worst possible of sins. From a theological point of view, the legalist declaration of one partner as " innocent " does violence to the doctrine of original sin in which all have sinned and fallen short of the glory of God. It provides a ground for self-righteousness alien to the mind of Christ. Also, such " loading of sin " on the back of one or both members of a broken marriage relieves other people and institutions in the community of responsibility for having actually contributed to the delinquency of the couple by either direct action, passive negligence, or feelings of fear and incompetence.

But the experience of both the church and the civil courts have attested that when *any* excuse is legitimatized, this is the entering wedge that continues to widen the breach until more and more excuses are allowed. Therefore, the idealist witnesses to the absolute ideal of Jesus for marriage and seeks to find the bases of repentance and forgiveness where this ideal has not been achieved, or, to use Fisher's fine insight, where the reality of Christian marriage has been violated, the couple may be brought back to the true condition of marriage.

The Forensic Approach

The forensic approach to the remarriage of divorced persons rests upon the promise that the teachings of Jesus refer to Christian marriage and not to marriage in general. Therefore, every effort must be exerted to determine whether or not the previous marriage of the person seeking remarriage was in deed and in fact a *Christian* marriage. Also, every effort of preparation and confrontation must be marshaled to see to it that the forthcoming marriage shall be Christian. The forensic-minded church and its minister raise several issues: Were the couple professing Christians and members of the church at the time of their previous marriages? Since their previous divorces, have they become Christians and demonstrated a faithful relationship to Christ and his church? Did they enter the previous marriage in good faith with the intention of making it last until death parted them? Were they sufficiently informed as to the nature of marriage at the time of their union to know fully and well what they were doing? Was the covenant of the previous marriage a defective one and therefore null and void?

The group that has had most experience and is most competent in the forensic approach to remarriage is the Catholic Church and its priesthood. To a great extent the Anglican Church has also exercised its casuistic efforts to determine the validity or nullity of previous marriages. To the Catholic Church, marriage is a sacrament of those who are baptized, although marriage between one baptized and a pagan is not sacramental. The priest is not the minister of the sacrament.

> The parties marrying are the only ministers of the Sacrament. . . . Consequently, those who contract marriage are the ministers, whether they are aware of it or not, even if heretics, who do not think that marriage is a Sacrament at all. Positively and unconditionally to exclude in intention the Sacrament from the contract would exclude the contract, and there could be no true marriage in such a case. (Henry Davis, S.J. [ed.], *Moral and Pastoral Theology,* Vol. IV, 6th ed., p. 66; Sheed & Ward, Inc., 1949.)

The Catholic Church reserves the right to decide whether a given marriage was in deed and in fact a true marriage or whether it is null and void. The nullity of a marriage is decided canonically after discussion, debate, and casuistic efforts to adjudicate between the eternal truth of God and the temporal dilemmas of the particular human situation. For this reason, "forensic" is aptly the name of this approach.

From the point of view of pastoral theology, the forensic approach to the remarriage of divorcees represents a double action: e.g., (1) determining the theological condition of the previous defective marriage and (2) reeducating and redeeming the couple in preparation for a forthcoming true marriage. This places the doctrine of redemption in its rightful relationship to divorce. One's doctrine of redemption cannot be subordinated to his doctrine of divorce. For example, take two persons, both of whom were divorced prior to having become Christians. As Christians, they fall in love with each other as new creatures in Christ. Can their purely pagan marriage prior to their having become Christian be considered as an impediment to remarriage? If one says yes, does he not at the same time say that this one sin of divorce remains untouched with forgiveness by their redemption in Christ? This is the kind of question which any serious pastoral theologian must ask.

Yet, on the other hand, when a Baptist or a Presbyterian takes such a position, is he saying in effect that marriage is a sacrament? Or is he saying that marriage is sacramental in one sense only, i.e., that the couple are each other's priest before God? They are taking and making vows that exist as an inviolable covenant between each other *within* the covenant of the broken body and shed blood of Jesus Christ. This in turn is what makes their marriage Christian. As far as their being Christians is concerned, this is what makes them married.

From this vantage point, Presbyterians, for example, have looked upon marriage performed by the church as being a covenant between Christians. Kenneth J. Foreman says: "It would clear the moral air in our country if all ministers would simply and flatly refuse to perform wedding ceremonies unless convinced that the bride and groom were each Christian in life and intention." (Kenneth J. Foreman, *From This Day Forward,* p. 3; Outlook Publishers, Inc.,

1950.) Also, Chapter XXIV of the Confession of Faith of
The United Presbyterian Church U.S.A., amended in 1953,
reads in part:

> Because the corruption of man is apt unduly to put
> asunder those whom God hath joined together in mar-
> riage, and because the Church is concerned with the es-
> tablishment of marriage in the Lord as Scripture sets it
> forth, and with the present penitence as well as with the
> past innocence or guilt of those whose marriage has been
> broken; therefore as a breach of that holy relation may
> occasion divorce, so remarriage after a divorce granted on
> grounds explicitly stated in Scripture or implicit in the
> gospel of Christ may be sanctioned in keeping with his
> redemptive gospel, when sufficient penitence for sin and
> failure is evident, and a firm purpose of and endeavor
> after Christian marriage is manifest. (James G. Emer-
> son, Jr., *Divorce, the Church, and Remarriage,* p. 127;
> The Westminster Press, 1961.)

Thus, the forensic approach to the remarriage of divorced
persons is not merely legalistic. It aims at the gospel as well
as the law. It uses the criteria of penitence, reconsecration,
and firmness of purpose in the endeavor of Christian marriage, as well as forensic attempts to determine the validity
or nullity of the previous marriage.

The Confrontational and Therapeutic Approach

The confrontational and therapeutic approach to the ministry of the church to divorcees seeking remarriage takes
the approach one step farther. It attempts to mobilize the
treatment facilities of modern marriage counseling and psy-
chotherapy to correct some of the underlying conditions
that predispose marital partners to later divorce. This approach consists of a combined confrontation of the couple
with the claims of the Christian gospel and their own personal culpability in the previous marital failure. Little or

no effort is made to fix blame or to declare guilt and innocence. The reason for this is made clear: all have sinned and
fallen short of the glory of God. Neither the former mate
nor his parents are solely responsible. We must work the
works of grace while it is day. No one is to blame, but
everyone is responsible. Thus guilt is not simply bypassed;
it is distributed. The church and its ministry share corporately in the sin. The lack of premarital confrontation
and counseling, the lack of pastoral follow-up of the couple after marriage, the absence of communication when the
marriage began to founder, and the loss of rapport when
the separation came — all these are a shared responsibility
between the church and the divorcee.

The second focus of confrontation and therapy is in the
establishment of a durable and responsible relationship of
trust and mutual goodwill between the church and its ministry, on the one hand, and the divorcee and prospective
spouse on the other hand. The church is not merely to lay
magical hands of blessing upon their marriage. The church
is to establish a program of counseling, guidance, rehabilitation, and therapy for the person who has been caught in
the bramble of human conflict known as divorce. This takes
time, patience, and a covenant of communication. If the
couple is willing to " follow through " with such a responsible relationship, then this in itself is a sign of maturity
which bodes well for the marriage. If they can carry through
faithfully with a covenant with the church and its ministry,
maybe they can also carry through faithfully with each
other. This is a fleece that must be put out. If the couple
stands this test, the possibilities for rehabilitation are good.

Beyond this point, the treatment of divorced persons is
the same for any couple coming to be married. The reflective pastor does not marry couples apart from their dur-

able and responsible commitment to the Christian faith. Whether they have been divorced is secondary to this. He does not marry couples on a hurry-up basis. Nor does he drop them in neglect after he marries them. He involves all couples in a durable covenant and in turn brings the oversight of the church to bear upon their total lives as persons. He provides them with guidance from the church fellowship in every aspect of their lives — in finances and Christian stewardship, in parenthood and preparation for Christian sexual union, in educational and vocational plans for their life's work in the Christian calling, and in intimate conversation about the burdens of guilt and unrequited regrets that they bring to marriage with them in need of confession and forgiveness. He relates them to a family physician from the outset. He encourages them to establish a personal relationship to a family lawyer. He introduces them to financial advisers and employers when appropriate and possible.

This confrontation and therapy characterizes the church and its ministers in their approach to *any* couple planning to be married. The person who has been divorced and wants to be remarried is no exception. This program, in line with the findings of the earlier portion of this chapter, includes several necessities on the part, not just of its ministers, but of the total church.

First, the responsibility for a position on these matters should be shared by the church and not left for the pastor to bear in isolation. Protestant churches, for example, by polity have room for maximum participation of the local church. Difficult cases should be shared with a continuing committee for this purpose. Matters of policy, *quite apart from specific cases,* should be devised by the committee and recommended to leadership and to the church as a whole as other matters of policy are decided. Policy should not be devised in an atmosphere of crisis, or upon an *ad hoc* dealing with one particular case, nor should it be the private decision of a pastor alone. It should be devised reflectively and should be a shared responsibility.

Second, the church as a matter of policy should require advance notice of plans for any marriage that is to be performed by the pastor. In the interim, the church can then provide guidance, instruction, and fellowship to the couple. The kind of discipline and instruction suggested in my pamphlet *Premarital Pastoral Care and Counseling* (The Broadman Press, 1958) can take place only when the church expects the couple to take these steps. This cannot be a private requirement of the pastor.

Third, the church should expect and enable their minister to become equipped educationally to deal effectively with difficult family conflict situations. He should be able to utilize the other technical resources of the community to meet the needs of the couple in trouble. Released time for special study should be made available to him. Pastors should be selected with this training in mind.

Fourth, the church should instruct, expect, and even require its members to present their family conflicts to some person or persons of their own choosing within the fellowship of believers before going to courts of law. The purpose of this should be stated redemptively and not punitively. The failure to do this, not the fact of marital trouble itself, should gradually become the source of moral censure.

The church and its ministry that has such an approach as this must be prepared to spend the necessary time to deal with the threats to the homes of the community of believers. They will occasionally be surprised to see how faithfully some divorcees will follow through with such attention and consideration of their need. They also will be impressed with how many couples do not have time to be bothered. They, as a church, will be called upon to perform the wedding ceremony of some persons who have been previously married. But the church marries only those persons who (a) take seriously the claims of the Christian faith for total commitment of their lives in marriage to Christ; (b) are willing to establish and carry through with a durable relationship of trust, reeducation, and therapy before marriage; and (c) who participate in premarital guidance, are willing to get all the technical assistance toward an effective marriage that the community can afford them. If a church faithfully holds to this, they will marry only one divorced person for every ten married by the church which marries " innocent parties."

In summary, the position set forth here is a combination of the forensic approach to marriage of divorcees and the confrontational and therapeutic approach. The laissez-faire approach is untenable. No church or minister worthy of the name of the Lord Jesus Christ can with a clear conscience and without the severest censure leave this problem alone, no matter how difficult it is. The idealistic approach is just that — idealistic, regardless of the semantic quibblings of G. F. Fisher. The society of today, two thousand years after the first radiance of the Christian community, is made ambiguous, not only by human evil itself, but also by the religious pluralism of Christianity itself. Some judicial handling of individual cases must be developed. The forensic approach to what constitutes a marriage must be combined with the confrontational and therapeutic approach. This seems to me to be the most realistic and courageous approach to take. This has been demonstrated to be creatively effective in the cases of the few divorcees who were willing to join in such a covenant and effort with me as a Christian pastor. I have had innumerable refusals of couples who went away sorrowing when confronted with the approach chosen here. Yet if a couple *will* follow through, much can be done to offset the damage of previous divorce and to prevent subsequent divorce.

One can agree with Pastor G. H. Hoffman when he says that the " remarriage of divorced persons under the ministrations of the church may therefore be permissible after full consideration of all the individual circumstances involved." But this is not in order to determine guilt or innocence of parties involved, for emphasis should be upon " the guilt of divorce and the sharing in it by all concerned rather than upon the legality of divorce or the distinction between a so-called 'guilty' or 'innocent' party " (G. H. Hoffman, " Divorce and Remarriage," *Lutheran Quarterly,* Vol. IX, No. 2 [May, 1957], p. 133).

Yet to consider all the circumstances from a modern confrontational and therapeutic point of view takes fifteen to twenty hours of careful work by a trained pastor. Many pastors who are either unwilling to devote this much time to a couple or afraid to attempt this because of a lack of training or both will refuse to marry a divorced couple. Then they will refer the divorcee to their brother pastor who is committed to a more time-consuming and disciplined approach. Many times the persons will be members of the church of the pastor who refers them. The only thing that the more disciplined pastor can do is to ask the couple to call him back later after he has had an opportunity to confer with the pastor who has referred them. Confrontation of the other pastor for his own irresponsibility is then in order! This is a part of the therapy for which the church itself stands in need.

EPILOGUE

These pages have been written to pastors, theological students, and laymen. The poignancy of the social problems that spawn individual pastoral counseling situations has been "the still, sad music of humanity" to which I have tried to be attuned as I have written. The reader may well have many questions as he finishes the book. My intention has been that this shall be so. For example, no ready-made, once-and-for-all answers are provided for problems such as these. To offer such is to misunderstand both the mystery of human suffering and the nature of the processes of pastoral counseling. Finality and finitude are contrary necessities of the pastor in all ages, and ours is no exception. If I had sought to say the last word on these subjects, I would have missed the Spirit of him who, when in the presence of the Pharisees and the adulteress, is said to have "bent down and written with his finger on the ground." This is symbolic of the temporary finitude of all writing. It is symbolic of the theme of ambiguity and dilemma that I have sought to use as a line of continuity throughout this book. If the pastor is not willing to bear the mystery of ambiguity and dilemma in the face of the mystery of human suffering, then he should reexamine the very nature of his calling. No one can do this for him. He alone must agonize with it before God.

Furthermore, the real question can be raised as to why I have not sought to deal with specific techniques of counseling. The plain reason is that I have done this in other works which I have written, and many other authors have dealt with these basic matters of the attitudinal orientation and technical procedures of counseling. In fact, the literature of the field of pastoral care is repetitiously full of such treatments. Consequently, I have chosen to deal with some of the transversal social problems that give context to the work of the pastor as an ethical man in dialogue with people before God. If there is one technique more important than the rest, here, it can best be underscored as the use of small groups, both formal and informal, both structured and unstructured, to open up closed minds and ventilate stuffy spirits, to cut down isolation, and to do away with the loneliness of both the minister and the parishioner. Such small groups frankly recognize the injustice of the institutionalization of preaching as a " religious speech " that is performed oratorically before a nonparticipating audience. Yet, at the same time, it activates what Wittenberg earlier called the " art of group discipline " whereby the group itself deals with the imperalism of any one member who might use the group as a soapbox without examining his own " hot certainties."

In the back of many pastors' minds is a real fear of small groups because they make the minister himself responsible on a face-to-face basis for what he says. But, also, pastors fear that small groups will get out of hand and run amok with clique formations and secret subcultures within the larger church. This points to the importance of vivifying already dead, dying, or otherwise useless organizations with new purpose and meaning. Usually, the attendance in these small groups is a problem to the pastor and to the few that do come, and effective implementation of small-group methods of pastoral counseling can both revivify and increase the attendance of such groups.

The security of a pastor or lay leader in using such methods can be enhanced considerably by continuing theological education at seminary and university centers where expert leadership and instruction are available. The following bibliography is a carefully selected reading list for specific attention of the reader for further study:

Bradford, Leland P., *et al.* (eds.), *T-Group Theory and Laboratory Method*. John Wiley & Sons, Inc., 1964.

Douglass, Paul F., *The Group Workshop Way in the Church*. Association Press, 1956.

Diver, Helen I., *et al., Counseling and Learning Through Small-Group Discussion*. Monona-Driver Book Co., textbook edition, 1962.

Gordon, Thomas, *Group-Centered Leadership*. Houghton Mifflin Company, 1956.

Hare, A. Paul, *et al.* (eds.), *Small Groups: Studies in Social Interaction*. Alfred A. Knopf, Inc., 1955.

Hollander, E. P., *Leaders, Groups, and Influence*. Oxford University Press, 1964.

Knowles, Joseph W., *Group Counseling*. Prentice-Hall, Inc., 1964.

Thelen, Herbert A., *Dynamics of Groups at Work*. The University of Chicago Press, 1954.

Wittenberg, Rudolph M., *So You Want to Help People: A Mental Hygiene Primer for Group Leaders*. Association Press, 1947.

As a pastor and teacher, I have wrought out my ministry in the midst of three great social crises which in themselves stand behind the problems discussed here. I would not be fair to my reader or to myself if I did not confess that much that has been discussed here is but the festering of the sores of the total body of society in our inability to deal with these three great sources and burdens of civilization. I entered the Christian ministry during the great depression, I began my first pastorate just as World War II broke out, and now, as a teacher, I teach theological students who are caught up in, contributing to, and perplexed by, an affluent society that overproduces both goods and babies and has not learned ways and means of distributing its own abundance. The judgment of God, as Elam Davies so aptly put it, today consists in our being weighed down by the very abundance and goodness of God. Therefore, the pastoral counselor of the future must come to grips with the mysterious challenges of population control, the threat and the fact of nuclear destruction, the possibility of another " great depression." These in themselves are meat for another volume. However, an honest author must admit to his readers that his knowledge has but touched the periphery of the great social problems of our day and yet thank God that his faith as a pastoral counselor has actually touched the hem of the garment of the Christ who stands triumphantly in his resurrection over against all that would separate us from him.